ANDRÉ JOHN HADDAD

FIVE HUNDRED DAYS OF KILLER VIRUSES AND ATTEMPTED WIT

Imagen Publishing

ISBN 978-1-9991072-2-2 (paperback)
ISBN 78-1-9991072-3-9 (ebook)

Cover & interior design by Aaxel Author Services &
The Creative Studio by Vee Vee

Printed in the United States of America

To Louise, my best advisor

March 19, 2020

Escape from Paradise

A tale of dread as we ran away from Spain.

It's Thursday 5h05 a.m. It's dark, a bit nippy, but we don't care. The adrenaline was doing its job. We've got to get there on time, we all said. Because the alternative was too awful to contemplate. Must get out of Fargo!

∞

Quarantine

We were in a voluntary quarantine and since last Monday, a forced one. The Spanish government established a countrywide total lockdown. Yesterday morning, we saw a couple scamper off with their suitcases. Secretly!

We've got 4 seats for Thursday morning's flight to Montreal, at 10h20 a.m. sharp. That's 6 days before our scheduled return. We're told to be at the airport at least 3 hours before departure. I crossed my fingers that

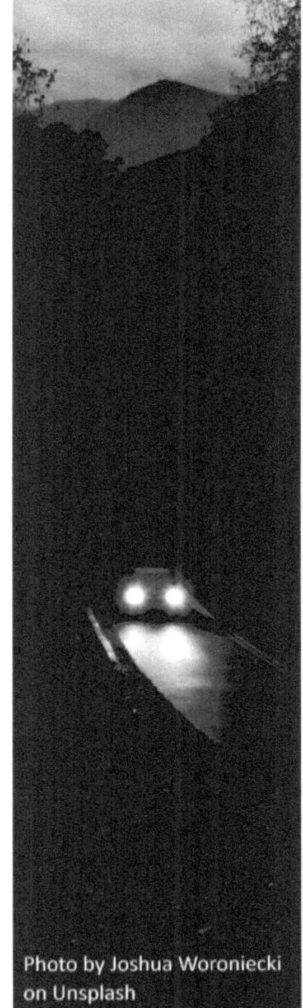
Photo by Joshua Woroniecki on Unsplash

the Spanish Police would not stop us *en route*. I'd heard the police were setting roadblocks. I'm thinking about this but... in my head only.

We're lucky to have 4 seats because our travel agent worked almost full time to find us the best possible way home: Malaga to Montreal, non-stop. Straight. Eight-and-a-half-hour flight in economy. In small seats built for Munchkins (the little people from the Wizard of Oz). But we really, really, really, don't give a... Because we're going home. Home sweet home. Home, where the snow falls and the sky is mostly grey. Yes, we honestly don't care, because home is where we have a politician (Premier Legault) who's doing his job like a pro. I'm proud of him. I'm so relieved we have Legault instead of President Gump. It's the first time I've been proud of a politician since Chretien told the Americans to fuck off, because he wasn't going to go to war in the Middle East. Our Premier, however, did declare war against the Corona. And we're all happy about it.

Be in Shape

I do have to say that our voluntary quarantine had its negative effect on our psyche. By the time we were ready to leave Spain, the Puerto Banus condo complex was almost empty. Living in a luxury apartment and unwilling to go out for air had generated a longing to get back home. Every time we felt a bit different (physically), we wondered if we had it. I'm sure you know what I'm talking about. So, we said to ourselves, when we get to the airport, we have to be in shape and we have to look the part. Be and look healthy, no coughing, no sneezing, no nothing -even though we've been coughing and sneezing in the morning for the last 10 years. Too much smoking will do that. So, we have stuff: Cepacol, Tylenol, Purell, gloves, masks... We will not give anybody the opportunity to stop us from boarding the aircraft because they think that the law has given them the skill to know who's OK and who's not.

We're Good to Go

Wednesday night, with our bags packed and ready to go, we tried to sleep. Next morning, 5h a.m. sharp, we woke up and got ready to go. It was dark outside. There was no one around. We left the apartment as clean as a whistle. Everything was spotless. It took all four of us, Michel, Andrée, Herself and yours truly, about 15 minutes to get ready. This is what I meant by the adrenaline was working overtime.

Taking the elevator down to the parking with 4 huge suitcases, I was thinking (in my head) that this wouldn't be a good time for a power outage. I know what you're thinking: I'm paranoid. No, not really. I always look at the dark side of everything as a precaution. That's not being paranoid. Paranoid is thinking that Justin Trudeau will be at the airport to welcome us back home.

But I digress.

The Big Bag Rover

We didn't get stuck in the elevator and we did succeed to jam the oversized suitcases in the back of the Big Bag Rover.

I was also thinking (in my head) about whether or not my Garmin GPS would bring us to the Airport or in the middle of nowhere… because it happened a week earlier.

Furthermore, I'm secretly hoping that our Land Rover doesn't die on us *en route* to Malaga Airport, which is about 60 kilometers away. I'm not talking about what's going on in my head because I don't want to scare anyone into thinking that it might happen.

So, I don't. We were finally in the Rover. It started. No problem so far. The garage door also opened. That's good too because we didn't know how to open it manually. Did I mention that I was also thinking about that?

In any event, Herself came back from the apartment having placed the keys in their proper place, as requested by the owner. I was hoping the police wouldn't stop us and demand to know where we were going at this hour. Remember, it was dark and there was no one around, not a single soul.

In the Rover, no one was talking. The GPS kept reminding me to turn left on Avenue de Lola something. We finally got to the Autoroute. Again, no one was around. And no one was talking.

The road looked unfamiliar. That's because we've only driven at night once. So, nothing is the same.

We were told to fill the car with diesel fuel before surrendering the Land Rover to Hertz. So, when is the best time to fill up? Not too early, and certainly not too late... Herself was looking out for rest stations with gas.

There was still no one driving the roads, except us. On our way to Malaga, we met about two cars and one truck. The airport seemed far away. Distant.

45 minutes later, we arrived at the airport. We found Hertz on the second floor *parkade*, and released our keys to a Hertz key box. The place looked almost empty.

So far, so good.

No power cuts, no car problem and, no GPS mix-up. A monitor showed our flight was on time. We're all wearing masks and gloves and I was always pouring Purell on my hands when not gloved.

Maybe you've noticed that I'm not talking about the Airline that sold us a one-way ticket for $1850.00. I'm not going to talk about it because Herself is ready to go to the Supreme Court if she has to. That's going to be another story for another time.

We also landed in Montreal on time. All we had to do is to get back home. We did. Montreal was still there, although there weren't too many cars on the road. It was spooky. Our friend Gilles picked us up at the airport. Finally, a friendly face. He drove us to Sainte-Adèle.

Home, sweet, home.

A

PS. From Joseph Heller: "Just because you're paranoid doesn't mean they aren't after you."

PS. As we landed in Montreal. I got a text message from KLM. Our Plan B was no more. Our flights from Barcelona to Amsterdam on the 25th followed by Amsterdam to Montreal are cancelled. Sorry, they said. No explanation. You're on your own. Hasta la vista baby! OK, now we really knew that Lady Luck was on our side. I didn't doubt it one single solitary second. I always look on the bright side of things when the going gets tough! That's who I am, I tell myself. Ask Herself, she'll vouch for me.

May 10, 2020

MI6 Encounter

Join MI6 and sign the UK's Official Secrets Act. That's all you have to do... and of course, keep your mouth shut until you die.

When writing speculative fiction, I often look for plausibility. Something that's engaging, interesting, but also as real as possible. Which brings me to two characters I developed for a novel called The Thirst.

Their fictitious names are Alexander Fionnuala and Willy Callender.

Both retired British government analysts, both members in good standing with MI6. Fionnuala is also a guest lecturer and journalist. He was born in Italy in 1936. Willy Callender or Wee Willy, is all about MI6 old school, a hands-on agent. He was born in Inverness, Scotland in 1943.

These book characters are fictitious but the two people I met aboard a ship cruising the western coast of Africa were very real. In real life, one lives on the west coast of the United States while the other makes his home

in Canada.

Some of the stories I heard were incredible, unbelievable and almost crazy. At first, Louise and I didn't believe a word. That is, until one day, as the sea calmed itself, the wives of these two old *wisenheimers* came up from their staterooms for a breath of fresh air.

Once the wives got together with their husbands, only then did Louise and I start to believe. It was a bit confusing because when comparing James Bond to these guys, you get the feeling that we shouldn't believe everything we've been told by the media.

We were together for a month aboard ship. I got to know them well enough to find them fascinating, and I wondered if I could keep in touch with them after our cruise came to an end.

It's important to note that they never, at any time, talked about the content of their work in front of me. If I happened to join them for a drink, they would respectfully change the subject, or at least clean it up, because they had both signed the UK's Official Secrets Act. Their contract with MI6 was for life. Retired or not, information was to be kept secret.

To make their point, they told me the story of an "old fart" who had retired 30 years ago from MI6. He had managed to be interviewed on BBC. He told his stories as if they were too old or unimportant. He was wrong. The "old fart" died of a heart attack a few months later.

Yeah, I know!

A

May 10, 2020

The Great Guy Laliberté Fumbled the Ball!

Through the Echoes is a sixty-minute multimedia show by artist Gabriel Coutu-Dumont. A creative device generated and guided to life by the procreator of the Cirque du Soleil himself, Mr. Guy Laliberté.

Set under a pyramidal structure, one is surrounded by lasers, 360-degree projections, kinetic video aerial scenery, atmospheric special effects and magnificent lighting. *Through the Echoes* is the first custom production for PY1, an original touring concept by Guy Laliberté and Lune Rouge Entertainment.

In order to properly set the context of my humble blurb on *Through the Echoes*, I must admit that I have seen the light. I have experienced the magic. I have witnessed LOVE, a Cirque du Soleil masterpiece. Thanks to Mr. Laliberté's genius, I will be forever grateful for his

part in making the world a wondrous place to exist.

That's the context. That's where I'm coming from. Now comes the bad news.

Through the Echoes gives new meaning to the word pretentious. An intellectual attempt to give meaning to our lives through flashes of light and loud noises. The final product of mingling man and technology is cold, unremarkable and fortunately, forgettable. As the lights were turned on to announce the end of the spectacle, a few applauded, maybe two or three unenthusiastic spectators tried to show some sympathy. My heart felt the pain of realizing that I wasn't the only one who felt dejected.

I didn't feel good. I was disappointed even though critics trashed the show a few days earlier. Nevertheless, I believed in Laliberté's genius. After all, I said to myself, critics bring very little value to the world. Regrettably, they were right.

I tried to understand how this show came to be. Didn't anyone tell Mr. Laliberté the truth? That bad is bad regardless of its creator's name or reputation? Wasn't anyone brave enough to tell the King that his new clothes showed him naked? That the King's new wardrobe was a con?

I'm tempted to say that *Through the Echoes* doesn't need a re-work. I have a mind to say that the show is fatally flawed and should be put out of its misery. I should say please, please, oh for God's sake, please.

But I won't say that. That would be cruel.

A

*PY1 is an innovative pyramid-shaped venue presenting unique entertainment experiences

May 10, 2020

You Think This Pandemic Is Horrible?

When writing fiction, I tend to get as close to reality without getting myself in trouble. So, talking about a secret city in the former USSR was a bit tricky. I wrote about the Russian Federation's Chelyabinsk Nuclear Facility, located in the city of Snezhinsk. To start with, Snezhinsk was known before the USSR's meltdown as a secret city. The Russians identified it as a closed town. It's located in Chelyabinsk Oblast, Russia, near the Kazakhstan border. You need a map.

Between 1957 and 1991, Snezhinsk was known as Chelyabinsk-70. Back then, the town couldn't be found on any map because it was a closed city and civil flights over the town were outlawed. We can assume that secret work was undoubtedly happening over there. One such possible activity was a military nuclear research program. No one was too sure about what was going on, but

Photo by Alexey Fedenkov on Unsplash

11

we could safely say it had something to do with the research and development of nuclear bombs.

Researching the town wasn't easy because few people had real information about Snezhinsk. Those who did talk to me about nuclear research (in general) were extremely discreet and didn't volunteer any information that would bring them close to a charge of treason. And, for the record, I didn't insist.

For that reason, I had to produce information on my own, meaning good old Google, Google Scholar and a few academic databases and search engines. The people I consulted with would tell me if I was on the right track or not.

It was a bit tricky but, in the end, Snezhinsk became an important as well as a credible character in The Jerusalem Cycle Trilogy.

A

May 11, 2020

A Filthy Little Secret: Why We Rely on Others to Manufacture Everything We Need

It's a filthy little secret!

It's the best kept secret I know of because no one's talking about it. No one's even thinking about it. No one!

What secret, you ask?

I can't tell you because it's classified. It's a dirty little secret because it concerns our most significant weakness as a nation. Our secret hides an important flaw: the wholesale decapitation of our country's most important jewel. We gave it away! We sold out!

Clues

I can, however, give you 2 clues.

Clue number 1: we need 7 million quick tests, but that will not happen any time soon.

Clue number 2: we need to permanently resuscitate our dead manufacturing capability to produce, among other things, PPEs (Personal Protective Equipment) and vaccines because this virus isn't going away. That too won't happen soon because universities don't teach Manufacturing 101. They do teach, however, how to export our businesses infrastructure offshore.

Ask yourself why does our handling of the pandemic seem so disorganised?

Is it possible that we don't have the manufacturing resources to fuel our strategies?

A

May 25, 2020

Unconditional Love, No Strings Attached

From my vantage point, a man with no children, I have a hard time explaining to myself the magic between grandparents and their little ones. From what I can see, the emotional bond between them is real and significant. I can understand the bond from the child's point of view: here's another adult who will love me and give me whatever I want! No questions asked! Now that, I can understand.

But what's in it for the grandparents?

Clearly, a grandparent has a specific role to play in society in regard to the raising of their own children's children. That's been researched and studied. There are good reasons why grandparents are so interested in the lives of their grandchildren. There's no doubt about that. But are there other more personal reasons? Motives that would explain more accurately why a grandparent's behavior toward his or her grandchild is so intense?

Here's my two cents on this subject based on close observation: grandparents are human

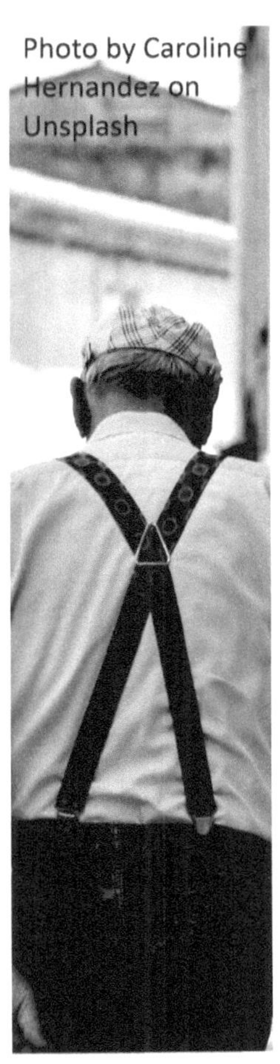

beings. No secret there. They need love and affection just like anybody else. In fact, in their later years, they probably need more love and affection than ever before. Seeing that their own children are busy with their careers, they have, at least in theory, accepted that their children have become adults with a life of their own. Their need to show affection toward their parents has shifted over the years toward their own kids and towards the community they live in. Unfortunately, grandparents are often forgotten, except when their services are required. More importantly, they are taken for granted.

Remarkably, grandchildren provide grandparents with a substitute. Young ones will give them all the attention, the affection and the love grandparents still need from their own children. Because everyone, that would include you and me, still needs to feel alive, happy and wanted, at any age.

When grandparents can see the end of the tunnel, life becomes precious. While their time is running out, their grandchildren keep reminding them that life can still be great at any age.

A

May 29, 2020

Another Freaking Reorganization!

I know, I'm repeating myself: the answers to our problems come from leaders, not structures.

Unfortunately, those in charge can't or won't hire real leaders because they want to control everything. They'll hire someone who'll take orders. God forbid a person would solve problems on their own! However, if control is not the issue, then the following paradox comes into play: do simpletons have the wherewithal to hire people better than themselves? Could they even recognize leaders if he or she bumped into them in the middle of the Sahara Desert?

The issue has always been about leadership. Not -another godforsaken reorganization. Not -a radio show announcer telling government what to do. Not -some big mouth on TV telling his public how he would handle stuff.

What I'm trying to say is this: it takes

Photo by Eugene Ga on Unsplash

real managers to handle what we're going through. Covid is a real test of our preparedness as a people.

So yes, we're failing.

But remember this: leaders can handle good, average and really bad employees. They can also handle good, average and really bad bosses. If they can manage, then they get the job done. They will find a way.

I'm sure you're asking yourself, "Don't we have good managers in key jobs?"

Well, sadly, no. Remember, we are failing the Covid Test.

That's the case because our business schools are doing a bad job at preparing people to deal with the future. They are letting anyone join their management classes as long as they pay the entrance fees.

Sometimes I wish we weren't born so stupid. It takes a lifetime to get to understand human nature and by then, it's too late because, more times than not, we don't give a damn.

A

June 1, 2020

Damn Backseat Drivers!

I hate them with a passion. That's basically what I want to say.

It's a bit surprising that people with no leadership experience whatsoever would have opinions on what our Premier is doing for us every day. I hear them everywhere. People bitching about this and that while standing in line in a big box store. I call them backseat drivers. The things they say tells me a lot about what's really going on: people talking about things that frighten them. And then, suddenly, they laugh about it, as if everything is going to be okay and then, to my surprise, they're saying there's nothing really going on. That it's all a lie. There is no such thing as the pandemic, they say.

Did I mention they don't wear masks?

Makes me want to shake them silly and ask them to shut up.

Then again, maybe I should keep quiet and let Mother Nature take care of them!

A

Photo by Taylor Deas-Melesh on Unsplash

June 2, 2020

Expedition to Montreal's Red Zone

We were preparing to leave in a few minutes. Last night, I checked the car's tire pressure and made sure the gas tank was full. I did that to make sure we made the least amount of stops along the way. Didn't want to be stranded in the middle of nowhere, especially in a Red Zone. Last week, in preparation for our journey to the big city, I had the Beast checked out. It's only a car, I know that, but it prefers to be described as the Beast, which, of course, it is. Anyway, it was in tip-top shape, ready to go.

We're minutes away from leaving our beloved hamlet of Sainte-Adèle. We haven't been to Montreal for well over 4 months. That's why we brought sandwiches, ginger ale, cokes, water and a second GPS. Of course, warm clothing was a must, just in case Mother Nature decided to recall Summer and give us a blinding snowstorm. Did I mention the Beast still had its winter claws?

The garage door opened; the Beast roared to life. It slowly made its way to the street. The garage door closed behind us as the alarm system

signaled us the AOK. I took a deep breath, made a silent prayer, and pressed down on the accelerator.

Did I mention we were wearing masks?

We were off. Our destinations:

1. Our first stop: meeting a specialist (doctor) in St-Jerome for an in-depth review of both our general conditions and bloodwork. Herself was eager to go on her next trip abroad, but it seemed no country was ready to open its borders, at least not yet. "Be prepared", that was Herself's motto. Mine was, "Keep the tank full."

2. Our second stop: the Laval Adonis, a great Lebanese food mart. We said we'd keep our shopping time to a minimum.

3. Our third and last stop: Herself's specialist dentist. She was located in downtown Montreal, in the heart of the Red Zone.

The Expedition

As soon as I reached autoroute 15, I initiated thrusters to operate the Beast at full power. The animal lurched ahead, scaring most little cars out of the way. I'm talking about German and Japanese crap-cars. The Beast ate them up like cheap chips. Predictably, the Beast was also allergic to Teslas. Too quiet. I mean, where's the fun in driving a muscle car if you can't hear anything? Sometimes I wonder what Elon was thinking!

A few minutes later, we reached St-Sauveur. I wasn't feeling too confident about the whole trip. But we didn't have any choice. I was trying to put on a courageous face because there was no need to stress Herself anymore than necessary.

We continued our expedition toward St-Jerome. When we reached our first destination, I asked Herself to stay inside the Beast until I had the time to check things out. Must absolutely stay away from Covid carriers because it's highly contagious, I said to myself.

As we left the medical clinic, the doctors wished us a safe journey back home. If only they knew! We had two more stops to do. Our examination completed, we drove through the hinterlands of old St-Jerome, Blainville, Ste-Therese, Boisbriand and, finally, Laval. Our second stop.

As we reached Adonis in Laval, we parked in an empty parking lot: a giant no-man's-land.

We filled our shopping cart with goodies from the Old Country as quickly as we could.

We set off for downtown Montreal. Our last stop. Coffee and cake at Herself's hygienist! Hardly. While cruising Montreal streets, we quickly noticed that the city was also empty of people and traffic. We saw very few humans walking the sidewalks. The shops were dark, restaurants were closed, banks still had a few clients waiting outside in the rain. It was unnerving. I had never seen the city so deserted. I had to remind myself that I wasn't in an apocalyptic science-fiction movie. This was the real thing. Worst of all, nobody knew anything about Covid except perhaps that it was killing our seniors.

Throughout our expedition, Herself hardly said anything. Neither did I. We finally reached our third destination.

An hour later, I thanked God. Herself was back from the dentist and was feeling relieved because she didn't need to come back for another 3 months. Setting aside her dentist's next treatment, we didn't know what would become of us. Would we be able to come back in 3 months?

On our way back home, Herself made her usual calls to friends while the Beast roared ahead.

90 minutes later, we were back home. At last! We were safe.

The moral of my story: even in the middle of a horrible pandemic, we found comfort at home. Surrounded by nature, life couldn't be better. So, I guess, there is no place like home!

A

June 6, 2020

The Narcissus: An Award for Self-Promotion

It's an award for this century.

Every year, thousands of ordinary folks would love to give a special award to those artists, politicians and CEOs who feed their narcissist pursuits by supporting a cause, demanding justice or lashing out against a wrongdoer ... with a song, a festival, a telethon, a gala, a series of tweets, a selfie or by way of an in-depth interview given on prime-time TV featuring themselves.

Why should they get a Narcissus? I think it's because they deserve it. Of course, not all self-centered individuals are narcissists or vain to the point of using a pandemic to bolster their ego. Of course not. Nevertheless, we can distinguish narcissists from us *normals* by the fake emotions they display to manipulate us. Lately, we've had a lot of fake testimonials from narcissists telling us how proud they are of those on the front lines of the pandemic. In reality, they couldn't care

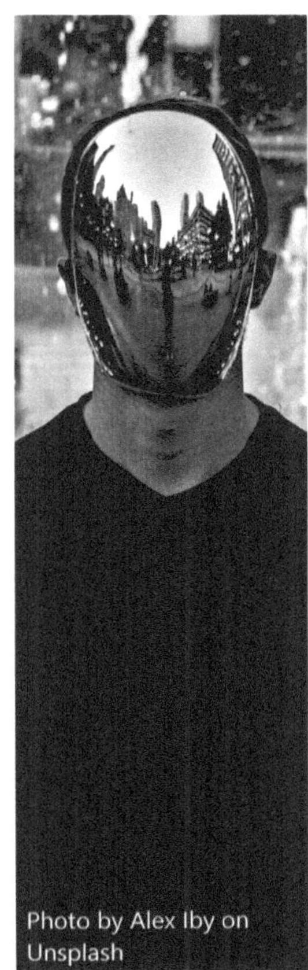

Photo by Alex Iby on Unsplash

less if these workers got infected and died in the process. They thrive on the pain of others because they have no soul. And there's no cure for that.

We are living in an age of self-gratification, from vanity to egotistic admiration of one's self, all the way to sociopathic behaviors.

Remember, everything the narcissist does is for the love of self, for his or her own image. He or she doesn't care if people get hurt in the process. By the way, they represent a little more than 1% of the population.

That's why narcissism is considered a real problem in most societies. What you see is not what you get. What you do get is completely fake, false, bogus and phony. Everything coming from the narcissist is sprinkled with lies and nonsense. As I said, a lot of people get hurt in the process, some never recover from these lies. I've had the misfortune to work in close proximity to narcissists. If and when I accidentally meet some of them, I'll do everything I can to quickly get as far away from them as possible.

Here's a tip on how to easily recognize them. They're like a black hole. They want to be the center of attention. Sucking the love of life out of everyone they meet is their trademark. Their need for attention can be overwhelming and sometimes criminal. Mental health professionals call them sociopaths.

Who do you think deserves a Narcissus?

Too many to list?

Go on! Start with just a few. Open your eyes. See through the disguise. Listen for the self-praise. See how they hurt people with their lies and fake tribute.

For your own sake, I really hope you can recognize them when you meet them.

A

June 18, 2020

When Things Get Tough

Listened to Mayor Plante (Mayor of Montreal) this morning on Arcand (most listened-to-radio-morning-man) on the issue of mobility in Montreal. I got scared pretty quickly listening to her respond to his questions, even though I don't live in Montreal any longer.

Her sentiment is that's she would rather be accused of doing the wrong things rather than nothing. Unfortunately, her things... cost billions annually. The thought of having this person handle billions of dollars coming from all over Quebec and Canada to run the city is simply frightening. It doesn't take an industrial psychologist to realize that Montrealers voted for a person of limited intellectual and leadership capacity. In our business, we would informally call her a "junior".

This lack of management skills in tough times reminds me of Minister Marguerite Blais (Minister Responsible for Seniors and

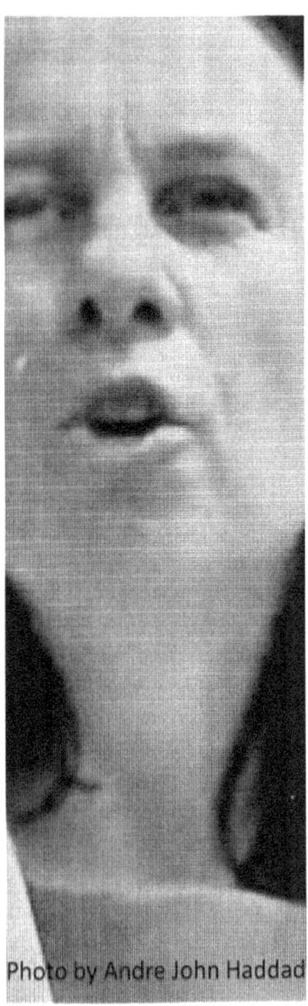

Informal Caregivers). But unlike Plante, Blais is a compassionate individual, although, in the end, both are incapable leaders. Both are incredibly weak and ineffective, especially when everything you're counting on is falling apart.

Sometimes I wonder why the really good ones stay away from politics. Maybe it's because they're not perfect and they know they'll get nailed to the cross for not being flawless. These days, "juniors" appear perfect for public office. They are naïve and inexperienced and expensive. Do they generally realize anything of worth? Do they accomplish tasks that pushed them beyond their limits to achieve important goals?

Methinks not.

What do you think?

A

June 18, 2020

Who's in Charge? Really... Anyone!

Photo by Haydn Golden on Unsplash

Who will keep our elderly alive?

The deaths of elderly residents in long-term care homes: it's a subject that has been in the making for many, many years. Our elderly are in real trouble and right now, we need a leader who will show the way.

It takes a crisis to see what people can really do. Unfortunately, Minister Marguerite Blais, although a compassionate individual with a heart of gold, isn't capable of handling the wholesale slaughter of our elderly by Covid-19. The Minister is out of her depth, meaning that Madame Blais is in a situation that is much too difficult for her to be able to deal with it.

Why Do We Have This Crisis in the First Place?

Unfortunately, while Madame Blais has been

pleading governments for years to treat the elderly with respect, no one has been listening. That's because she wasn't a threat to anyone. She still isn't because that's not who she is. She wouldn't know how to apply pressure on someone if her own life depended on it. She's a good soul, and in normal times, she would be a good figurehead. Now, our blatant disregard for our old folks is staring at us. I'm ashamed of myself for not doing more. I'm also ashamed of you too.

Firsthand Observations

Louise and I visited our parents and family every week, 2 to 3 times a week, for about 10 years. That did not include hospitals visits, doctors' appointments, etc. We felt we were their protectors, their advocates. Almost every time we would visit them, we would ask ourselves: who cares about these other residents? Where are these other people's sons and daughters? Who fights for them? We didn't do anything beyond this questioning. We cared, we lost sleep over our parents' welfare, we managed their situation, but our social conscience ended there.

Let's face it, we, as a nation, don't really care what happens to our elders. They're old, often times weak, they need constant attention, and it's hard to help them. We don't want them to be a burden. We like them silent, almost invisible.

Now that we, as a society, have hit the proverbial wall, we're waking up to our worst nightmare: they're dying because of us. We simply didn't care. If we had, we wouldn't let the government put the likes of Blais in charge of this problem. We need someone who is able to get the Premier to listen and to put the money in the right projects. Someone with clout. A person with courage and intelligence who understands how to leverage power. A real advocate.

Hardly the Top People

Let's agree that the people responsible for our elderly are not the top people we find leading the Finance, Health, Education portfolios or the Conseil du trésor (Treasury Board Secretariat). No, we've put in place good people, honest people, but people with no political influence, people with no political savvy nor political leadership.

Today, the real Minister Responsible for Seniors and Informal Caregivers is, of course, Mr. Legault himself. Our Premier. Does he have to do everything?

I'm really sorry to say this, but Madame Blais has to go.

A

June 23, 2020

The Internet Crash: Coming Soon to Your Neighborhood!

You think the Covid-19 pandemic is horrible? Wait! See what happens when the Internet crashes. If that ever happens in your lifetime, you'll think Covid-19 was a mere walk in the park.

A few years ago, I listened to William Daniel Hillis talk about how the Internet will, sooner or later, crash.

∞

The Very First Internet Phonebook

He remembered a time when he was listed in the very first Internet phonebook. Printed on real paper. He was one of a few hundred who was networking with fellow scientists on what is called today the Internet. By the way, Hillis is an American inventor, entrepreneur, and scientist, who pioneered parallel computers and their use in artificial intelligence. When Hillis was on Ted-

Photo by Vinicius Marques on Unsplash

33

Talks, people listened.

He said something to the effect "Why don't you prepare yourself with a Plan B. A plan that will permit your organization to function, especially when the Internet crashes."

I think it's fairly realistic to think that the Internet will crash, because everything that goes up must inevitably come down. It's called gravity. In this case, I call it Human Nature because, whether by accident or not, eventually the Internet will crash and paralyze the world or part of it, for a significant period of time. Someone will make a mistake or simply unleash a digital bug. It doesn't really matter whether it's accidental or not. It's bound to happen. Not because the Internet has grown out of human proportion, but because, sooner or later, crap happens. Just remember that eventually, everything deteriorates, breaks down, collapses and eventually fails.

Plan B

Hillis said: be prepared. Build a Plan B: a system that will permit your organization to communicate with others, manufacture products and provide services to the population or to your clients -without the Internet.

If you happen to work in a hospital, an airport, a school, a trucking company, a bank, a supermarket, the police, the army, a Broadway show, a singer, a surgeon, a nurse or priest... your activities might grind to a halt and not know why. People will lose their livelihood and many will lose their lives.

Is it too early to talk about the imminent demise of our beloved Internet? Should I postpone this conversation to next year?

Yes?

No?

Oh! You're saying you don't believe that can happen!

Now that's a real shame.

A

June 23, 2020

A Mysterious Character

"The little one was a mystery. Very few were born so stunning, so happy and so incredibly magical. The young mother of fourteen immediately gained prominence within her village and the region." I started to write about Naples (Italy) a few months ago. This chapter is set in1800 BCE, in the present-day location of Nola, a municipality in the Metropolitan City of Naples.

Those were my first words in a new novel I had planned to write about Naples, a city dating to the 2nd millennium BCE. Not knowing clearly where my words came from, I made a decision to keep on writing.

∞

Origin of Characters

A few months before the pandemic, my godson, his wife and child visited us for Saturday brunch. Louise had prepared braised lamb.

The little one was seated at the table and was busy having lunch. That's when it hit me. The little one was my godson's daughter. A precocious bundle of joy. Her energy and incredible curiosity were the source for a mysterious character in my book about people living near Vesuvius.

While thinking about the little one, I asked myself if all my characters stemmed from real life or were they mostly the product of my imagination?

Short answer: I don't have a clue.

A

July 5, 2020

Hiding the Biggest Secret in Plain Sight

Everyone has secrets. That's no secret. We have them because we don't want anyone making judgements on who we are or what we've done. We also hide them deep. So deep that sometimes we forget we have those damn secrets in the first place.

Tell you what: I have a secret I'm willing to share with you. But only if you promise to keep it to yourself.

Promise?

I'll take that as a yes. So here it is. You're not going to like this because it's not only my secret, it's also yours. In fact, we've all been hiding this secret since we were born. We're afraid to talk about it or even silently think about it because, well... because we're afraid. Maybe if we don't think about it, it'll go away. Like magic.

But it won't, it never does. It's always there. In some deep corner of our mind, lurking in the dark, waiting.

If you really want to know... my secret is

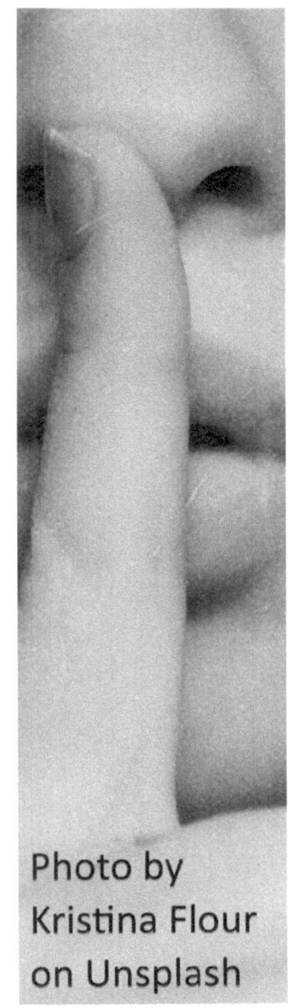

Photo by
Kristina Flour
on Unsplash

that I really don't want to die. Not only now during the pandemic, but for the rest of time. I'll do anything, I say to myself, to stay alive. Really!

Of course, that's not quite true because I smoke 2 Havanas a day, eat raw meat and drive too fast.

I know, I'm full of contradictions and secrets. That what makes me so charming! Maybe!

Fact is, I know I have contradictions. But I'm also one who likes to help others even if they didn't ask for my help. Like today. I thought you'd feel better if someone, like me, told you what I was going through with my f.....g secret. To tell you that you're not alone, and whether that helps or not, at least you'll know that you're not the only one living with THE secret. A secret hiding in plain sight.

I've got other secrets, of course; so do you, for that matter. But, let's agree to keep those for another day.

Okay?

A

July 6, 2020

Don't Go Pointing Fingers at Me, Not Anymore!

No more finger pointing! Okay?

Young people blame us for the state of the environment. Fair enough. I can live with that accusation and try to do my best to change my polluting ways. So, yes, we have to clean our act! Sure, the environment today isn't what it used to be! So naturally, it's about the survival of our species! I agree with that. No ifs, ands, or buts. It's my commitment.

Unfortunately, in light of young people's recent behavior during the pandemic, I feel they have lost the credibility and the right to criticize my generation. At least until Covid-19 finally disappears from the planet.

Young people can and should keep on talking about the environment. For as long as they want. They shouldn't stop or hesitate. Because we as a people, old and young, are not suicidal. However, young people pointing their accusing finger at my generation is from now on, *verboten* (banned, disallowed, prohibited and forbidden).

From this day on, I really don't care what they have to say about me and my generation. They lost that privilege.

I feel it's a sad state of affairs when a generation of young people has so clearly showed its true colors during this pandemic. That hue is made up of two letters.

M and E.

A

July 12, 2020

Being respectful is a lot more difficult than you think

I respect people who stand up for their rights. Usually!

Even those who refuse to wear masks or get fully vaccinated, because it infringes on their God-given right to die an early death or to contaminate and kill someone else through their complacency. Again, I try to respect people's opinions, no matter how wacky they may sound.

Bless their little hearts.

If you're one of those freedom fighters, you should congratulate yourself for doing a great job at protecting our rights. By taking a stand that nobody in his right mind would take, you've shown us that there is always another way of doing things. Being logical or listening to science is but one path. No Sir, you're no follower.

For my part, I wear the mask and got twice vaccinated. I've been wearing masks for the last two and a half years aboard planes. By the

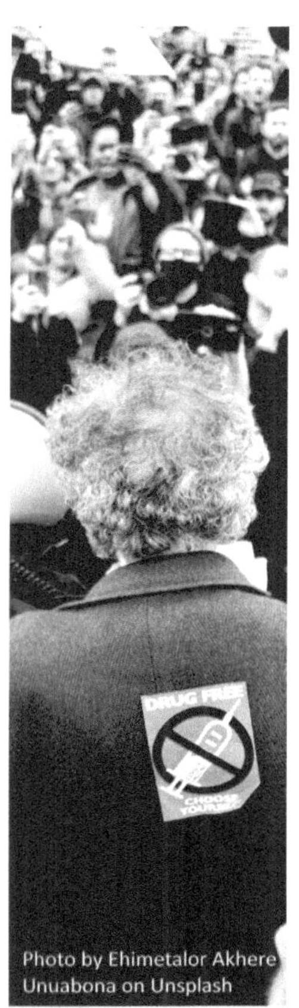

Photo by Ehimetalor Akhere Unuabona on Unsplash

way, wearing the mask reminds me of when I was a little boy. I wore masks back then, in fact two: the masks of Zorro and of the Lone Ranger. Felt good to be an avenger.

Anyhow, may God be with you.

Really, you'll need it.

A

PS. You should also protest the washing of hands while you're at it. Shouldn't waste a good protest!

July 28, 2020

Patriotism: It's Not a Canadian Topic

Most, if not all Canadians, love their country. We display it in different ways, but it always comes down to a sense of belonging. Where we live... is our home.

Unlike Americans, we don't display our patriotic fervor in public every second day. Likewise, we don't profess that God is exclusively on Canada's side. What's more, we rarely tattoo our national flag on our faces. We do, however, show our respect for our country every time we follow rules, laws and traditions. That's our way.

Which brings me to patriotism: it's not a Canadian topic. It's there, but we don't make a big fuss about it. And we seldom argue about whether some of us are patriotic or not. As I said, it's simply not a topic.

Lately, I have been asking myself if I was patriotic. Compared to Americans, I guess not. However, I will admit that I'm proud to wear the red maple leaf pin when I'm abroad.

But the question is now being asked, and rightly so: are we patriotic when so many

Canadians are battling the Covid-19 virus?

Are we patriotic, or are some of us following the Trumpian playbook of offensiveness and disrespect? Have we understood that, as a nation, people have to care for other people, for the good of the nation? Being patriotic is not about waving the flag. Is it not to gently and respectfully wear the mask and to wash our hands so that others will survive the virus?

A

August 2, 2020

I Admit It: I Was Addicted to Hockey!

After 26 years of no hockey, meaning the Montreal Canadiens haven't won a Stanley Cup in over two decades, I finally began to watch the new season.

I wanted to be impressed. I pleaded with the gods of hockey to let the Canadiens win... something. Anything! I tried to keep my eyes open and not fall asleep. But, in the end, I failed. I fell into a deep, comfortable slumber.

Then a voice called to me. "You know they're going to eventually lose?" it said. "One or two lucky wins don't make them Stanley Cup champions!"

"No, no, please, don't say that!" I said sadly.

When the dust settled, I finally came to my senses. All the sports commentators' drivel about what will or could happen will not make a poorly managed team come to life, especially when the top brass doesn't have a clue, not one single original idea of

Photo by Taylor Friehl on Unsplash

how to win.

The top brass does, however, know how to sell hotdogs and beer, condos and parking spaces. But that's about it. Because when it comes to hockey, they are as clueless as two short planks. They have shown us through the years what they are incapable of capturing: the cup. We know, however, that management is always responsible for the success or failure of any organization, whether it be in sports, manufacturing or show business. The boss makes it happen or not.

So, what's my point?

The official position of the Losers' Association for Montreal Exhibition Sports (LAMES) has been quite clear: there isn't a professional team-sport in Montreal that will or can win.

You can't argue with LAMES. They know their stuff.

Go, go, losers!

A

August 6, 2020

Are we witnessing the end of Lebanon?

After years of war, occupation, chaos, corruption and devastation comes... the end.

When I saw the two explosions on CNN, I was horrified. However, for all conspiracy buffs, a word of caution. This event was not due to a terrorist attack. Not by a long shot. Consider instead, a slow decline of order, of discipline, of civilization, of the rule of law and of common sense set against the onslaught of constant political rivalry, historical interference from the Egyptians, Assyrian, Babylonians, Achaemenid Persians, Greeks, Romans and Sasanid Persians empires and of course the West, which should include the Americans, while not forgetting the Russians and the Chinese.

With the incredible build-up of corruption and its by-product of chaos, as well as a flawed constitution crafted in 1943, I believe that the inevitable implosion of the Middle-East is a work in progress. The extinction of a region, several civilisations and their people,

Photo by Marten Bjork on Unsplash

are part of a scenario that has been evolving non-stop since we've begun to write our history on clay, papyrus, animal skin and paper. The implications are terrifying: generations of good people who, over the last 3 to 5 thousand years, have never had a chance in hell of living and prospering in peace and within the rule of law.

I asked Louise what was wrong with me. Why wasn't I heartbroken? How come, a Canadian from Lebanese descent, only 3 generations in Canada, couldn't shed a tear over the slaughter of innocent men, women and children? Why?

It took me a while to get my head in the right place to understand what was going on. Then, it came to me: a few years ago, I wrote a Trilogy entitled The Jerusalem Cycle. The story is about the near destruction of the Middle-East and World War 3. I wrote the story because I believed that this scenario was more than probable. Today, I believe that it will happen. I understand the reasons why the destruction of that region of the world is a real possibility. I wrote about it through the eyes of a terrorist, but it could also happen by accident. An accident like the one we've seen on TV. An accident that only happens when corruption perverts everything it touches.

This week, we've all witnessed the accident. There's a chance that the Lebanese people will not be able to fix their country. I'm saying that because it's more than broken. The people of Lebanon, from all descent and religions, are fed up. Beaten. Tired. Depressed. I think it's fair to ask the question of whether Lebanon, as a nation, is on its deathbed? I don't know. But the forces behind every accident, every single attack on Lebanon are still at work, poisoning the world with religious and political ideology. These forces will inevitably make the Middle-East the center of the world, for all the wrong reasons and for the whole planet to witness. It's like watching a locomotive going full speed ahead toward a mountain that will not give way.

At this point, I must call on your good sense to remember that history is not about the past, it's about what will happen. That said, I'm sorry. I'm really sorry because the region's fate has been in the works for thousands of years. Right under our noses. *But can we stop it?*

You know that's not the right question. You're too bright to be fooled by something so simplistic. The real question is quite different: *Do we want to save the Middle-East?* Now, that's a better question. I feel it's the right question because... don't you think we all know the answer?

A

PS. To all the people who want peace, my kin, my uncles and aunts, my cousins and their children, I suggest we pray. Get on our knees and plead mercy. Because this one needs a miracle. I hope you believe in God and that He or She is listening.

August 26, 2020

I Told You So! I Did, Over and Over Again.

It's been 27 years!

On August 2, 2020, at 3:23 PM, I wrote that the Montreal Canadiens would lose. Well, they did, eventually. I hate to say it, but I told you so. On many occasions.

Now what?

Whatever happens in an organization is management's responsibility and, in this case, it's the Montreal Canadiens management's fault.

They have been failing for almost three decades.

When will top management admit defeat and sell the organization to people who know how to win! Let's start afresh!

A

PS. While we are at it, let's also fire every sports journalist in Montreal. And start over!

PS. I use the word journalist in jest, but of course, you know that. They are but simple noise makers.

Photo by Yifei Chen
on Unsplash

August 29, 2020

Braindead weather Anchors

Do they train them to be absurd? Perhaps a seminar on the illiterate grasp of our world.

Did I ever tell you that I love weather anchors, especially when they have to give us the bad news:

1. it's going to rain
2. it's going to snow
3. it's going to be very hot
4. it's going to be really cold

Sad Faces

When that happens, they put on a sad face. A sympathetic grin appears on their mugs because they want us to know they feel bad about telling us the weather's going to be awful. After all, they're just messengers. It's not the weather anchor's fault if the weather is evil! Nevertheless, the anchor almost wants to apologize on behalf of Mother Nature, who

Photo by ThisisEngineering RAEng on Unsplash

happens to be, on occasion, very bad.

I'm so, so sorry about the weather! Look at me! I'm carrying an umbrella! Or snowshoes! They say mournfully.

They want us to believe they are empathetic to our plight. We might, after all, melt under the hot sun, drown in a puddle of water or freeze to death if we happen to go outside in February.

You know what? I'd like to put a frown on my face too: the frown would signify that weather anchors really don't understand that Mother Nature does what it does because we live on a real planet, not in some TV reality show.

My sad face should also express a wake-up call. Look at the world and thank God we have rain, snow, wind, hot and cold weather because, hold on to your hats, we live in Canada, on planet Earth. This is real! It is what it is because it's a planet. And the weather or the planet doesn't need to be forgiven for anything.

We need you to tell us what's going to happen so we will be able to make a decision on how to dress, whether we should take the train, plane, car or metro. Or maybe just stay home and think like an adult.

Dear weather anchors, you should try it sometimes: to act like adults. And more importantly, to treat us like adults. I promise you'll feel good, and more importantly, so will we!

A

October 2, 2020

He's Not Perfect!

Yes, our prime minister is not perfect, but he's the one at bat. I will respect the man no matter what. I don't have to agree with him, but I will stand fast. He's all we have and for that reason, we better help him do his job. If you can't or won't help our prime minister, hold your tongue for a few more months until a vaccine is ready. Yes, it means to quiet yourself and, for godsakes, stop bitching.

Yes, yes, I know what you're going to say: it could take a year. Or more. Sure, but nevertheless, persevere and show others what you're made of. We are a strong people. We've been through a lot, and I've seen what we're capable of achieving when we put our minds to it. I've witnessed it firsthand. We are made of strong stuff: the stuff that doesn't back down, doesn't give up or show signs of weakness.

Premier Legault is doing what he can with the information he has. I've been following what other leaders are doing around the world, and Legault is dealing with the virus with what he has at his disposal.

The virus is a wake-up call. I said a few months ago that there would be a second, a third and a fourth wave. With each wave, we will learn and we will adapt. We will also learn not to repeat our mistakes and we will also learn more about our systemic weaknesses as a country and as a people.

A

PS. It's a myth that young children can't wear masks! Our teachers can make that happen. They know how. They know why. Teachers are the architects of our future. They mold young minds to think. They can also help us because masks are for everyone.

One more thing: front-line employees of our health system are our real heroes. Not actors, not singers, not comics or TV personalities. But we just can't help ourselves! We ask our fake heroes to comment when, in reality, we should be asking our front-line heroes what they are going through... every day... to remind us, to enable us, to take a step back and thus provide perspective.

October 4, 2020

"God Wants Trump..."

A middle-aged woman from Wisconsin said, "God wants Trump to have a second mandate". She voiced her opinion to a CBS seasoned reporter. "I'm afraid that's not true, Madam," the journalist said. The reporter paused because he most likely didn't know what to say next.

But I do. Because you see, here in Sainte-Adèle, Quebec, I speak to God every day. It just so happens that He told me a few months ago that He doesn't interfere in our business down here on Earth. He's too busy monitoring the unfolding of His universe. Whatever that means!

But, he warned me: "Don't use My name under any circumstances."

I asked him why He was talking to me in the first place.

He said I was special.

Sic...

A

October 8, 2020

Sleepless in Sainte-Adèle

It's no surprise to anyone that COVID-19 is having an impact on our psyches. It's pretty difficult to deny the obvious. This virus is no joke. And it's real. Covid-19 means that a correction is being orchestrated by a tiny virus no bigger than a thought. It's a game changer. It's a killer. It won't go away like magic, which means that life post Covid-19 will be different and not necessarily in a good way. Yeah, I know what you're going to say: change is good because... yada, yada, yada. Well, to be honest, I don't like change or Covid-19 and I certainly don't like surprises. I could go on about buying my own Christmas gift and wrapping it, but that's for another day.

Okay. I get it. I know change is real as well as inevitable. Maybe some good will come out of Covid-19, but right now, I don't care. I also know that we'll have to live with the changes Covid-19 will bring about, whether we like it or not. But way down deep, in the farthest recesses of our brains, there are little boys and

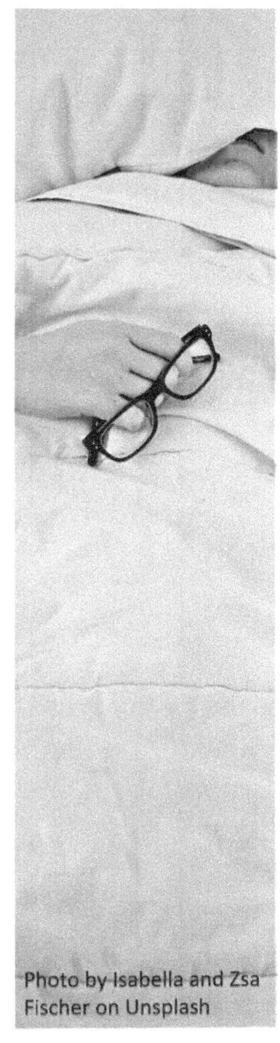
Photo by Isabella and Zsa Fischer on Unsplash

girls trying to see if they'll be able to get past Covid-19 in one piece.

I, for one, am having a difficult time falling asleep. It's no big deal because eventually I do. But still...

Luckily, I found a way out. A solution. A sure-fire technique to nip this problem in the bud. And it's free.

Last week, I happened to wake up to Google's radio-alarm. I was just about ready to start my waking day when Paul Arcand passed the mike to the sports commentators. It wasn't long before I fell into a deep, relaxing sleep. Later, I asked myself what happened?

The answer was surprising. If you want to fall asleep, just tune-in to whatever radio show asks your brain to listen to senseless commentaries about who should be wheeling the hockey puck next season.

This is what happens: our brains, out of self-pity or self-preservation, immediately shuts down. Like a circuit breaker. At that very moment, when our ears hear the words hockey, football or soccer, something wonderful happens. As if by magic, we're dreaming again. Just like that! Our brains are saved.

But don't take my word for it. Try it.

Sports commentators will be the last voices you hear before falling asleep. To be honest, just knowing I'll be listening to them makes me go directly to REM state.

Now, isn't that amazing! What do you know! Sportscasters do serve a useful purpose after all.

Happy dreams, you lucky people!

A

October 29, 2020

A Mickey Mouse Diagnostic

Not again! A diagnostic for the birds.

According to The Canadian Press, 700 doctors from 50 hospitals say centralization, as well as a lack of onsite managers, have caused multiple deaths in Quebec hospitals during the health crisis.

It could have been 7000 doctors saying the same about centralization, and it would still be a bad diagnostic, an inept attempt to explain why the system isn't working. Even though many doctors have held the position of Minister of Health and Social Services in past years, the problem of efficiency persists. For what it's worth, here's my diagnostic.

Over the last 40 years, I've had the privileged of working with centralized and decentralized organizations from around the world. I've learned the following:

#1 Centralized organizations can be as efficient as decentralized organizations and vice versa.

#2 Centralized and decentralized

organizations can also be inefficient and display the same operating problems.

#3 The common denominator for a successful organizational structure is the quality of its leadership: the people at the helm of these organizations.

#4 A good leader makes any kind of organization structure work well. An incompetent leader renders all types of organizations inefficient and causes harm.

So, what's my point: doctors are very good at helping us live a healthy life. That's a given. That's their job. I literally trust them with my life. But there ends my trust because they have not been trained to make a diagnostic of complex organizations and how they work.

The "Good Doctors" are pointing their fingers at the wrong culprit: the wrongdoers in this case are the top managers put in charge of these so-called centralized organizations. They have the responsibility to make an organization work. They work in a unique position to facilitate, enhance, inspire and help their resources do the best possible job. And that is regardless of the structure of the organization.

When an incompetent leader is at the head of an organization, he or she will impede, discourage and damage the organization he or she is responsible for.

So please, stop Mickey Mousing around and point your accusing fingers at the people who are really responsible, those at the top, the senior civil servants in the health network. They are clearly not doing their jobs. They are, in fact, damaging the system.

Imagine, all this inefficiency can be turned around in a few weeks. It just takes the right people to lead these organizations toward efficiency. Men and women with vision, leadership skills and a whole lot of courage to tell bureaucrats to do their jobs quickly or get out of the way!

A

PS. To all front-line health care personnel, thank you very much. I mean it. I've seen you at work and I know what it's like working for an "inhospitable" management team. Stay resilient, be strong and healthy because we need you.

November 1, 2020

Resilience: What to Do in 3 Easy Steps

How to get it and how to grow mentally stronger is not that much of a challenge.

∞

But First, What is Resilience?

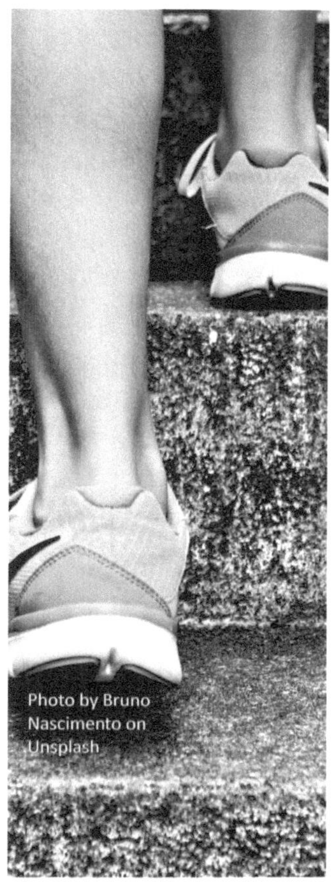

We all know that life is about dealing with expectations and setbacks. We generally succeed in life by not letting the world have the best of us through endurance and perseverance. Some people call that strength of character. Over time, we adapt. We learn to survive life-changing and stressful situations, such as Covid-19. The trick here is not to let our fears win over our ability to succeed, no matter what.

Everyone is experiencing the virus differently. Covid is one of life's twists and turns. Okay, it's a big one! Facing the unknown, or the displeasures of not always getting our way, is all about becoming a better human being. There's no short-cut or pill that will spare us from the growing pains we all go through. It simply doesn't work that way. Life can be wonderful as well as hard. Never easy. However, each time we learn something new and keep our heads above water, we build resilience. We get stronger.

So How Do We Get Resilient?

I'm not going to talk to you about theories and beliefs, or values. Let me just suggest a few practical things I've done to manage stress and generate a bit of resilience.

1. When I feel down, stressed or just lousy because the world isn't unfolding the way I'd like, I do something physical: I walk, run, do the Dyson vacuum, play tennis, shovel snow, clean the yard, run up stairs, dig holes, plant something... I generally get off my ass and stay active for as long as I can. Sometimes I hate doing that, but I really don't have a choice if I want to feel better. There's a minimum: 30 minutes a day if you're over 50 and fit. If you're younger and fit, consider a minimum of 2 hours a day of physical activity. It may not help you solve your problems, but it will give you a break. It also helps to become physically stronger. It builds strength as well as resistance to pain. That's step 1.

However, that's not enough. Remember, there's no silver bullet available, just hard work and the will to go through this f.....g pandemic in one piece.

2. Now the healing part kicks in. So, you're physically in better shape. That's a must. It's not an option. Let's move

into second gear. For that, I usually talk to someone: a real person. Someone I trust will listen to me and generally be a good friend. Choose that person wisely. He or she must be strong and have enough experience in life to be patient and non judgemental. We're talking here about venting. Some call it bitching, but it works. Venting our pain and frustrations out loud alleviates tension and stress. Texting is not venting! It's not physical enough. Venting will, for at least a short period of time, make you feel better. When I do that, I feel I can see the light at the end of the tunnel. There's hope, I say to myself. Venting helps me get rid of some of the pain just long enough to get a good look at my problem. That's step 2.

3. Now, I start thinking about my next step. Feeling a bit stronger, having had the opportunity to have a conversation or two about it (again, no texting, but a face-to-face talk, in person with masks, or on a cell or a computer, through Zoom, Skype, Team... whatever works for you). Then I start thinking about how to solve my problem. The issue is and will always be, what's under my control. What can I change that can help me get through another day, another week, a few months, and so on. Little things can add up to a solution that really works in the long run. That's step 3.

Those 3 steps, combined, generate resilience and are a necessary routine for life! It's a routine for mental health, for human beings of all ages.

Warning

A word of warning: if you tried really hard and still don't feel any better, see your doctor, talk to your parents, grand parents, friends or get professional help from mental health specialists. Don't take no for an answer. Get help, get better and then help everyone around you get through this pandemic... in one piece.

A

November 4, 2020

Theft Right under My Nose

Theft and racketeering on a small scale at your supermarket are probably the norm.

Yesterday, within 15 minutes, I witnessed two separate events: theft and attempted theft. These events should tell us something about an organization's failure to manage and supervise their human resources. Of course, you know that the losses incurred by supermarket chains will be summarily handed over to you, the consumer, in the form of price increases. In that light, a 2018 report of the Canadian Retail Council estimated that shoplifting accounted for more than $5 billion a year.

Here's a bit of context to better understand what 5 billion really means. Five billion dollars translated in numbers is made up of 9 zeros ($5,000,000,000). You could spend $25,000.00 every day for more than 500 years (that's 182,500 days) before you would run out of money.

Breaking it down even farther, it means you would have to spend over $500,000.00 every day for the next 25 years in order to spend all that money.

What really amazed me was how 3 employees openly participated in these thefts. For Sherlock Holmes aficionados, this following clue should help you understand what really happened.

The first event was at the fish counter. There, two employees were at work. One employee generated a sticker price after another employee weighed the product I had chosen. Then, with a big smile on his face, the first employee added more product, free of charge.

A few minutes later, at the checkout counter, a client openly complained about being charged for a product that the store cashier would routinely not charge. The store employee, seeing that I had clearly understood what the client said, was caught between the client wanting a freebie and me! The cashier stood motionless. She said nothing. There, behind her mask, I could just imagine what was going through her head. She avoided eye contact with me as well as with the other customer, who at this point, was still openly complaining that she had not received her product for free! I'm sure by now that you also understand that the customer is also part of the problem. The customer was pushing the cashier to commit fraud in front of a witness. Try to imagine what this employee would say to that customer if she had the chance to do so in private. I would love to hear that conversation.

In my experience over the past 40 years, I had to come up with diagnostics that would explain why small and large organizations all over the world were routinely losing money. Unfortunately, fraud, theft and racketeering would rear its ugly head more times than not.

In all likelihood, these 2 events mean that a lot more is happening in this particular store, leading me to believe that there's a racket possibly happening over there. A racket requires that more than one person (a team) is actively stealing. For that to happen, store employees would be working without real supervision. Which then leads me to believe that some of the management staff at this store are somehow involved, hence enabling a form of racketeering.

Please remember that theft, or shoplifting, means that more dollars will be spent by consumers to buy what they need for their families. Somebody has to pay, and that somebody is always, always, always... you.

A

PS. If you think about this, who do you think I should call tomorrow and inform them of what I witnessed? The store manager? The store manager's supervisor at corporate? Or somebody else higher up? Or, then again, just let it be? What do you think? How would you handle this?

November 8, 2020

Less Covid Is Better: Isn't It Obvious?

Less Covid-19 means more money in our pockets. Isn't that evident?

I'm wracking my brains out trying to understand the balancing act between Public Health and the Economy our government officials are managing every day. I'm also trying to make sense of those who insist that wearing the mask is an infringement of their God-given rights as citizens. That the measures the government is taking are unfair. That these measures are destroying our economy and our liberty.

Well, it seems obvious to me. Less Covid-19 means more money in our pockets.

I try to understand, I really do. I struggle to appreciate the other person's point of view. I also want to believe that people understand what they're doing as well as the consequences of their actions. It's kind of easy for me to say that the sooner we get the Covid virus under control, the faster the economy is going to recover and grow.

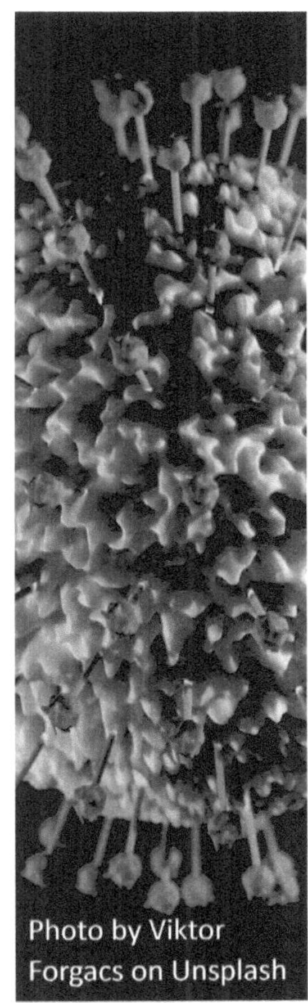

Perhaps, an even stronger economy may come out of it… if we play our cards right.

It's obvious! But saying that is a bit disrespectful because declaring that something is obvious makes other people uncomfortable because they may not get it! What's obvious to me may not be so clear to another. The whole obvious thing is not really conducive to building understanding and a consensus. Maybe I need to explain my point of view.

Okay, so let's assume that it's not that obvious. It's not even clear. There's something missing, some kind of clarification that directly links Covid-19 to my wallet, to jobs, to building the future for our children.

Trying to balance Covid-19 and the economy is a mistake. There's no balancing act necessary; in fact, it's counter productive. I feel there's a gross misunderstanding of what's at play and what we have to do. Half measures don't work. If you have a headache, you don't take half a pill! The era of half-measures is coming to an end. "In its place, we are entering a period of consequences," noted Winston Churchill.

Here's my understanding so far.

1. A pandemic kills economies. Kills jobs. Kills savings. Kills wealth. Kills futures. Kills retirements.
2. Kill the pandemic. No, that's not enough. Crush the pandemic. Devastate the virus. We need to be angry at the virus, not the people trying to manage it.
3. Crushing the pandemic will very quickly generate a stronger economy because we'll be at work again. It will produce new manufacturing capabilities. It will create new jobs and the money to pay bills. It will generate wealth for the people. It will strengthen the retirement of our senior citizens.
4. What we do, individually and together, to crush the virus, will directly impact our wallets, the prosperity of every single man, woman and child.

How do we quickly kill a pandemic and, at the same time, quickly rebuild our economy?

The answer to that question should by now be obvious, right?

A

PS. Dear Prime Minister, it's time to take the gloves off. We are ready. Don't hold back! Don't take any prisoners! Don't show mercy toward the virus. It's time to attack and crush the virus. The enemy needs to be destroyed. Forget the balancing act. Again, give the virus the final *coup de grâce*. Quickly. You've shown us that you know what to do, especially now. This is not only a medically based strategy, it's common sense, and it's absolutely about leadership.

November 13, 2020

Running Loose in the Streets

The deinstitutionalization of the mental health care has had too many casualties to deny their existence. Why did that happen:

1. a horrifying misunderstanding of human nature
2. a scandalous burden on families
3. a strategy to save money that backfired financially, socially and legally
4. an invisible problem facing us everyday

A Little Background

Starting in the 1970s, our government realized that public spending in the health services was growing twice as fast as the gross national product, a common problem shared by Europeans and the US. So, someone had to come up with a drastic reduction in public spending. The Minister of Health and Social

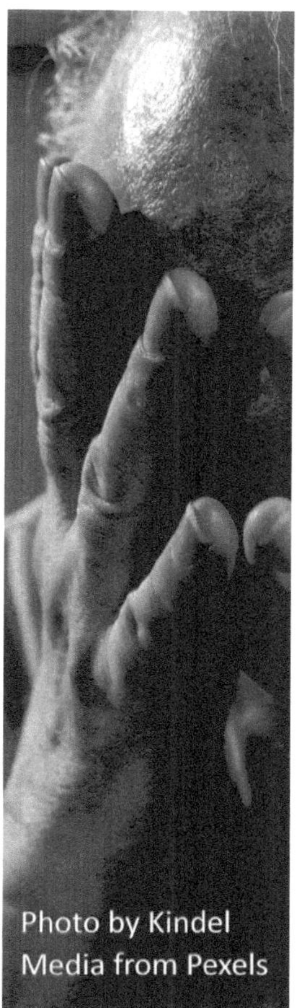

Photo by Kindel Media from Pexels

Services, under the Quebec Liberal government (1989-1993), proposed the following objective: Let's give citizens the services that we are able to afford. So far, this makes sense.

The thinking back then was that deinstitutionalization would enable the rapid and effective resolution of physical, and more importantly, psychological health problems, thus avoiding long periods of hospitalization. For the mental health community, this implied the development and implementation of new ways to take care of people within the community. Right here! This is where I have a problem.

Negative Consequences

The negative consequences of a financially based strategy to deinstitutionalize mental health care are incredibly simple to explain: the required community-based follow-up was not and is still not available. And it never will because we'd need to care for that to happen!

So now, we're stuck with governments, one after the other, that refuse to acknowledge that we have moved our mentally disabled from the despised institutions to the streets. That's where they end up when they decide not to take their medication. People with mental health issues can be treated with the proper medication but, no one can force them to take the magic pills. That's the law. In a way, I can't blame them because medication dulls the spirit.

Families

The families are caught in the middle. The cops don't know what to do with them. Hospitals treat them for a few hours or days, and then push them out onto the streets as soon as they can. This revolving door system has no end. There's no real solution in the pipeline. Just pain and grief and frustration... for everyone involved in helping those in need.

Didn't anyone tell the Minister that his 1970 strategy would fail because it was based on faulty premises:

1. that the community could help them get better!
2. that doctors, nurses and family members could follow-up and make sure that they would be taken care of.

I think a lot of people said the same thing 50 years ago. I'd bet they were told to shut up.

What am I trying to say?

1. for one thing, we don't need prisons for the mentally ill
2. we need more humane institutions where we can really take care of the mentally ill
3. we need to change the laws and make families able to commit their loved ones when they go... excuse me for using the following expression but it's the only one that fits, when they go crazy and are dangerous to themselves and others
4. accept our failure with grace and start building "humane institutions"

Let's get the people who display mental problems and refuse to take their medication off the streets. Please!

A

November 16, 2020

A Request from My Cousin

My cousin asked me if I could write something about professionalism. I found the request a bit odd but soon came to the conclusion that it could be a challenge, especially these days, when professionalism has lost its attraction in favor of easier behaviors that everyone would find more entertaining. So, here goes.

∞

Professionalism

"We need a pro," they would say seriously. "This time, we can't afford to fail." They were in trouble. "We've invested too much to money with amateurs. We've tried and failed, over and over again."

So, what are they talking about? What do they mean by a professional?

For some, a professional is characterised by his honesty, reliability and competence. Professionals also display a high level of

Photo by Linas Drulia on Unsplash

maturity, confidence, as well as a reputation to match. They are known to listen to people before making a diagnosis or a recommendation, and they are generally well-mannered.

For some, being a professional includes doing a good job, even under extreme pressure. They are serious and respectful. They possess specialized skills and academic training and sometimes they hold rare and specialized knowledge.

They have a deep personal commitment to developing their own skills. Professionals have generally mastered a specialized knowledge needed to succeed. They become, with time, a reference in their industry. To achieve that level of notoriety, professionals keep their erudition up-to-date in order to continue to deliver the best results. At a certain moment in their careers, they are recognized as leaders in their field of endeavor.

Generally speaking, professionals get the job done. They're highly reliable, they never give up and they keep their promises. If they can't deliver, they will recommend resources who can. They will always attempt to make things right.

On the whole, professionals don't make excuses but focus on finding solutions. As I said, they keep their promises and they can be trusted. They will always do the right thing regardless of the consequences to themselves. Professionals take responsibility for their actions.

Reality Check

The definition of professionalism presented above is an attempt to get a good grasp of what it takes to be a real professional. Unfortunately, the text above is part wishful thinking, part fiction and part untrue. Anyone that has displayed all of the above is probably a saint and therefore quite rare and probably deceased.

Fact is, pros come in different shapes, different shades and they rarely resemble each other. So, what am I trying to say? What do they have in common?

To become a pro (one is not born a pro), and be able to do whatever is written above, one needs to grow. That's it! It's the only element that we can generally agree on that defines all professionals. They have learned through years of toil and experience to become professionals.

Yes, you guessed right. It's a destination. An on-going struggle and a challenge.

A

November 19, 2020

Planning Christmas during the Pandemic

Or how a strategic plan for your first Covid Christmas holiday might be handy.

What is a strategic plan and why do you need one this year? Simply put, a strategic plan sets a destination or where we want to end up and how we're going to get there. The plan should be organised and methodical. A way to identify the steps that will get us to our desired end point.

Now let's talk about your Christmas.

If you don't have a holiday plan, you'll end up anywhere. And that's okay if you don't care where you wind up. It's like taking a trip and flipping a coin at every intersection. Again, that's okay.

However, if you feel there's uncertainty ahead of you, for instance, that you can't really be sure the vaccine will get in your veins in the near future, then you need a plan.

Here's an example that you can use to build your own strategic plan for the holidays, especially after you finally realize that, in any case, family gatherings should only happen a

Photo by Ravi Patel on Unsplash

couple of times a year.

I call this plan, "For heaven's sake, when are they leaving?"

Objectives:
1. I want to meet as many family members as I can.
2. I want to meet them in person, in my home.
3. I want to make sure no one gets sick, including myself.
4. If necessary, I want family members to stay a night and leave the very next day.
5. I want people to get along all the time.

Steps:
1. I will invite groups of 6 to 8 people to my house for the holidays and I will specify a time and date.
2. The invitation will stipulate that they would need to be free of all virus symptoms for a week prior to coming to my home.
3. The invitation will stipulate that no one should bring food or pets to my home.
4. Washing hands will often be required during their stay at my house.
5. Children will be monitored by their parents at all times.
6. Those who don't believe that the virus is real will be asked to keep their opinions to themselves. There's also a promise made to me, in writing, to go into therapy right after the holidays. I will talk to them beforehand and make sure they understand that they need help, but, and in spite of everything, I am really looking forward to their visit.
7. Tylenol, Pepto-Bismol, etc., will be available to all adults during their stay at my home.
8. A gift list will be provided to all family members as to what I would like and not like to receive for Christmas and / or New Year.
9. All gifts should be vetted by my wife.
10. As Christmas should be a happy affair, no family members

going through difficult times should accept my invitation. I will talk to all family members beforehand and make sure they understand if and why they should stay home.

11. Although we all love Christmas music, holiday tunes will be limited to 1 hour (or less) every day.

12. Smoking is allowed everywhere in my home except in the kitchen and the bedrooms.

13. My cigars will not be available to anyone but me. So, I will advise family members to bring their own, if they so wish. However, only Cubans will be allowed to be smoked in the house.

14. Anyone not comfortable with my requirements will nevertheless be able to share our family reunion through Zoom, Team, Skype... A Christmas card will do as well.

15. No distressed or ripped jeans nor lumberjack attire will be tolerated.

16. No fruitcakes. It doesn't matter how old they are.

17. No conversations about religion, unions, Trump, money, your job, sports, Vlad the Impaler, and the virus will be tolerated.

18. CNN coverage of the US election will be limited to 15 minutes per day.

19. Christmas mass will be streamed through Netflix or Amazon Prime.

20. On Christmas and New Year, only happy thoughts will be permitted. Smiles will be required at all times.

21. My destination: Checkout time is set at 11h am the next day; family members will be provided with a choice of box-lunches (chicken, ham or vegetarian) as well as a non-contact goodbye kiss.

Merry Christmas.

A

November 25, 2020

Diego Armando Maradona Franco Dies and Sportscasters Cry!

Football player Diego Maradona died from lifestyle choices while health worker Maria Mariangeli died from Covid-19.

Guess who gets a statue?

Maradona was an Argentine professional football player. He was believed to be the greatest football player of all time. From 1984, Maradona did cocaine. They say he died from his lifestyle.

His fellow citizen, a 43-year-old Argentine health worker named Maria Mariangeli, died from Covid-19. She was one of many health care professionals who died while caring for people who found themselves in desperate situations.

One died from self indulgence while the other died from dedication. Of course, you know as well as I do that Mariangeli will not be remembered. She will never have a statue erected in her honor.

I just heard that some sports journalists,

here in Montreal and around the world, were weeping because Maradona died too early.

Really?

I can't say what's on my mind because it wouldn't be nice or respectful.

However, I would like to say the following to sportscasters: get your head examined!

A

November 29, 2020

I Was Right!

I wasn't paranoid or fastidious! I knew this would happen. And it did!

A few years ago, we added a garage to our home because that's what we've been doing since we bought the house in 1982. Our house is a work in progress. We just add space to our house to store more stuff. Nothing new there. Men and women have been working on their homes ever since the expression "*might as well*" became part of the human experience.

Our last project was going to be our last, but today I can assure you that this was just wishful thinking.

Let me come to the point, which is all about dealing with construction people: no matter if you're right, no matter if you say it over and over again, construction people will almost every time do what they think is best rather than execute a request from their customer. They'll listen to you. They'll smile and say, "Hey, you're the boss." But they don't mean it.

Case in point. We were told that with all the

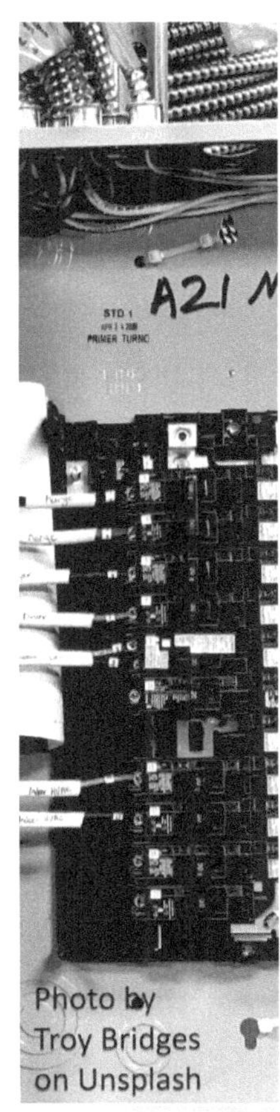

Photo by
Troy Bridges
on Unsplash

money we were putting on this addition to our home, we should wire the electricity from the street to our home... under ground. No more ugly wires coming from the street to an ugly electric pole sticking out of our roof. "No more! Not necessary," they said. "We'll take care of it."

"Okay," I said. But, more importantly, my wife said, "I don't care. Just do it." This is a guy thing.

With that mandate from high above, I told the contractor that he should go ahead with whatever is needed to get our electricity underground and out of sight. "By the way," I said, "Could we also install a parallel system to allow me to introduce new technology to the house via an underground passage? And, why don't you prepare for at least 4 lead cables, pre-installed, so we could just pull the new cables or whatever new technology we require by just pulling a cable that would be attached to the new tech."

"Sure, but you don't really need that because we can simply fish the new cables through the underground passage in a matter of minutes." (Technical terms: Fish Tape or Electrical Wire Fishing Tape). Their contempt was almost palpable.

I said, "No. That's not what I want, because when I'll be ready to introduce new tech to my home, you won't be there if and when it doesn't work out!"

I told the project managers, told the electricians, told everyone individually and in a meeting where they were all sitting at the same table, that I wanted 4 lead cables, now and in different colors. I wanted that now as in the present era, at this moment, promptly, straightway... I left them and I believed they had understood.

Today is Sunday. More than 5 years later. And I'm now prepared to introduce new tech to our house by fishing a new cable from the street to the house.

With the help of one of the people who introduced new tech to my house when we were adding the garage over 5 years ago, today I wasted 7 hours trying to fish a cable through the underground pipe. The key word here is "trying".

It didn't work. Of course, it didn't. Why should it?

In fact, the fish-tool is still in the underground pipe, and we are unable to pull the-fish-out!

In the end, I must admit, humbly, that I was right. I wasn't paranoid or fastidious. I had predicted the future 5 years ago. I did that with so much accuracy that it leaves me... frustrated because I let it happen.

But I was right, damn it!

Still, it's no consolation to be right because I realize that I was wrong to believe that an industrial psychologist could communicate clearly "what the hell I want" from his contractor and from all the other construction workers. I was wrong to believe they'd listen. I was wrong to believe it would be a good idea to be pro-active! I was wrong on so many levels that I now feel responsible for not camping at our house 5 years ago and personally overseeing the digging and trenching of my underground technological freeway!

Wrong, wrong, wrong!

If God is listening to me, I swear I will never do that again. From now on, I will always supervise.

Then again, who am I kidding!

A

issue: when a fan becomes a nonbeliever.

Enter Mister Geoff Molson

While waiting in a downtown office for my turn to meet the person I was scheduled to talk to, there, sitting behind his mask, was Geoff Molson himself. I recognized him immediately. He was also waiting. In person. In the flesh, so to speak.

While pondering what to do next, I asked myself if it would be okay to tell him that he should fire his Executive Vice-President and General Manager Marc Bergevin because he is living proof of what Albert Einstein said, "The definition of insanity is doing the same thing over and over again but expecting different results."

I thought about that and decided against it. So, I came up with another angle.

What if I said that at 72 years old, I had limited time left to see the Montreal Canadiens win the Stanley Cup before my time on this planet is up? I said to myself that I had a pretty legitimate reason for asking because you know... we're all hemmed in by the clock going Tick-Tock, Tick-Tock... relentlessly.

I got a phone call and forgot about the whole thing. I rose and found a place where I could talk. I didn't want to bother anyone with my conversation. Once my call was done, I proceeded to the coffee maker and accidentally ran into the man.

I asked him if he had 2 minutes to spare. He was kind enough to say yes.

"I just wanted to tell you that... I'm 72 years old."

He looked at me, trying to understand where I was going with that. We were both wearing masks, so reading people might have been a little iffy for both of us.

"It's just that I don't have too much time left to see the Canadiens win the Stanley Cup," I said politely.

I saw him thinking again. Then, looking down, he said, "Well, we have a very good team this year..."

I said, "Thanks".

He answered, "Don't mention it".

Meanwhile, my *esposa* was looking at us. A week later, she told me that she knew why I had approached him.

I said, "And...?"

She didn't answer. She simply shrugged, and that was the end of that.

I'm sure you want to know what else he told me.

Well, I'm not saying, because it's secret and confidential.

And that's the end of that.

A

December 7, 2020

Mental Health Care Is Not Really a Priority

Well, it's moving day in Montreal.

A fire broke out at a homeless campsite in downtown Montreal. Residents pressured City Hall to relocate the homeless. City officials encouraged the homeless to move into one of the city's living quarters rather than camp out on public land. The timing was perfect. The city now had a legitimate reason to act: safety. Monday morning would be moving day for the homeless.

Amid the homeless that have fallen on hard times because of the economy, Covid or just bad luck, there are between twenty and thirty percent that require more than humane lodging. Some require treatment, supervision and constant follow up. For those requiring chronic psychiatric care, there is no place to go. That's because we have, as a society, decided that mental health care within the community is the best environment to get better. That strategy hasn't worked out. The word you're looking for is failure. As I said in

Photo by Matthew Ball on Unsplash

an earlier text, there's this merry-go-round that the mentally ill go through: streets, prison cells and hospitals.

Mentally ill people don't get the care they need because we have abolished what used to be called mental asylums. Families, police and hospitals are now trying to cope with mental illness. They are not equipped, nor are they responsible for treating the mentally ill.

I don't believe the community is the best place to heal the mentally ill. We called it deinstitutionalization. It's a strategy that was based on money, not on the treatment people required.

Forty years ago, we made a mistake. Yet, we still refuse to recognize our past blunders. Our incredible lack of lucidity is partially responsible. However, the real culprit is our political correctness when we use human rights as a pretext to do nothing.

The pain the mentally ill endure and the grief they cause to others are real.

It's time to re-open care facilities for the mentally ill. It's time for the politicians to shape the new laws required to treat the mentally ill. It's time for the courts to listen to family members who are afraid for their lives. It's time to listen to the police and hospital workers who babysit the mentally ill, because they have nowhere else to go.

Listen. Act courageously. Heal.

A

December 17, 2020

For Pete's Sake, Get a Grip!

Leave your problems at the door and respect employees. Is that too hard to understand?

Just dropped by the local gas bar for a refill.

Went inside because I needed a carwash code.

Photo by Tom Ramalho on Unsplash

And there she was, listening to a woman scream her bloody head off because someone forgot something or other back home. She was screaming at the cashier, a woman who, by now, I am absolutely sure, is the best person a business could have to service their customer's needs.

Over the years, I got to know her pretty well. She smiles, she remembers who you are, what you want to purchase; and she's efficient. She also has children and a life outside the store. She's a lady with a good heart and great customer relation skills. She's the real deal.

She was crying. "I can't take it anymore," she said desperately.

I tried to help her, but the damage was done. I told her that we could talk after Christmas. I tried to reassure her by telling her that my wife and I were both industrial psychologists and that we'd be happy to help. She said thank you.

Now, I know we all have our own problems to deal with. We also have bad feelings or emotions that include sadness, anger, and fear. We experience them because we're human. Your problems are real and true. But for heaven's sake, let's not hurt the people who are doing their best to provide us with a service, whether they are Health care workers, Cashiers, Gas station clerks, Waiters and Waitresses, Sales reps, Bank clerks or Security personnel. Remember, they also have their own problems to deal with -including minimal wage. Remember, they have families, children and yes, they too have issues.

They don't need your problems or your inexcusable bad temper and lack of respect on top of their own troubles.

So, be a good person and get a grip! Even if it's only for a few minutes. Give employees a freaking break and respect them. Leave your problems at the door.

It will surely help employees go through the holidays unscathed, uninjured and undamaged.

That could be your Christmas gift.

A

December 19, 2020

Acquittals: Getting Away with Murder Has Never Been This Easy!

Two acquittals almost the same week. And before you say it, there are no coincidences in this life. No such thing exists. Everything happens for a reason.

Two white men, one charged with rape and indecent assault and the other with sexual assault, forcible confinement and harassment. Believe it or not, both men were acquitted on the basis of reasonable doubt!

No, that's not what really happened. Reasonable doubt is just the icing on the cake. The real cause is organizational. These two men were acquitted because, in both cases, prosecutors didn't have the time or the resources to properly prepare their witnesses and present their cases. I prefer to believe this explanation rather than accuse them of incompetency. That would be unfair and false.

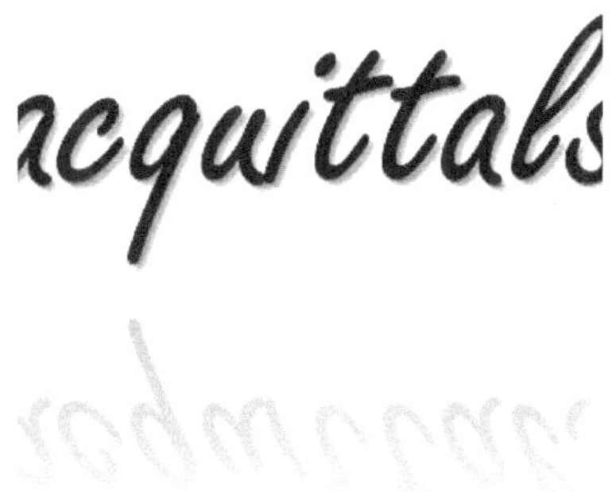

Photo by Andre John Haddad

So, please don't point your fingers at them. If you need to know who's responsible, please look higher in the hierarchy. No, look higher. Look at all the past and present Ministers of Justice: they have systematically under-resourced prosecutors for decades.

The acquittals didn't happen because the law is not appropriate. It's because we, as a people, don't put our money where our mouth is.

In both cases, the judges didn't have any choice. They had to work with what they had.

In both cases, the people, that's you and me, well, we lost a bit of confidence in our justice system. That's been happening for some time now.

So, the acquittals are not accidents.

A

December 25, 2020

Alone on Christmas

What happens when you're alone on Christmas day?

I asked myself that question a few days ago. How would I go through the Holidays alone, without my Louise? At first, I didn't want to answer that question because I was afraid of what I would find out. But I had to because there are too many people out there, alone, or with someone that doesn't care. I think it's our job to do something about it.

The answer to my question is simple and terrifying.

Something starts to rip your heart apart.

If the loneliness lasts too long, we get into real trouble. Trouble as real and as bad as any trouble a human being can go through.

So, this is what I do. It's not something I'm used to doing because... well, I don't. But now, with this freaking virus, I figured I had to do something. I started calling people I know who are alone and find out what they're doing. I joke around, I try to be funny, I talk about how

Photo by Daria Pimkina on Unsplash

the future is looking brighter. I make conversation.

Basically, I make contact while being as sincere as possible. And you, did you get someone to smile today?

A

December 28, 2020

Let Me Propose a New Word for HR Professionals

My! My! Look at him inventing a new word for HR to use on a daily basis.

This time of year, linguists from all over the world review new words that have taken hold in a people's language. Inspired by American politics, I said to myself, why not try my luck at inventing a word. A term that would say everything about our time. Is that even possible you ask?

I thought about it for a long time and I came up with this one. My new word is **sociopathetic**, as in... *He's in a sociopathetic class of his own.*

I've joined together the words *sociopath* and *pathetic* to provide a new meaning and depth to someone's horrible outlook on life on the job. I feel HR people would

appreciate my new expression when helping managers focus their feedback in the most constructive way possible.

I'd like to believe that my word should be enshrined in the HR prototypical* library, a word used within a vocabulary used to describe a type of deviant's job performance.

Sociopathetic. Remember that word. It might come in handy.

A

*Prototypical - first example from which all later forms of said behavior can be delineated.

January 3, 2021

Incredibly Naïve Article on How Democracies Will Bounce Back from the Trump Era

A good friend shared with me the Presencing Institute's article entitled "The Darkest Hour Is Just Before the Dawn" by Otto Scharmer. The author discusses how to transform Trumpism after Trump. The article is well written and appears, at first glance, honest. Scharmer provides us with the strategies required for democracies to bounce back, better in fact, as well as bounce forward, with trust and truth. His words, not mine.

I can't imagine a better article on the topic if you didn't care or dare say something that everyone is afraid to hear. And what would that be? Why did certain democracies fail to uphold decency and replace it with lies and the ensuing chaos?

Photo by David Everett Strickler on Unsplash

Naïveté

Scharmer's article is an exercise in naïveté and, in some way, a blatant lack of honesty and intellectual discipline.

Please, let me explain.

I'd like to put it as succinctly as I can: Trumpian chaos is a natural by-product of sociopathy.

As a consultant and industrial psychologist, I worked for and with sociopaths. As a writer, I wrote about them in my books. Whether we know it or not, sociopaths are in our lives. They create confusion. They lie. They hurt people. They can be found everywhere: in business, education, politics, law, religion, finance, families... And they are close to us. Some can be highly visible, while others are more discreet. What they all have in common is their lack of conscience or their absence of remorse. Some would say they have no soul. In my experience, all encounters with sociopaths end badly. You can't win with a sociopath.

Scharmer's article fails miserably because it doesn't start with the identification of the chaos-virus. Not the man, but the man's condition. In this case, the malady or the disease is sociopathy. Let me remind you that sociopaths are not quite human: they cannot be fair, loving, generous, truthful or just. They are a malformation of the human species; they represent narcissism in its purest and foulest form.

Next time anyone feels like telling you what to do about restoring normalcy between people, let them start with the root cause.

Now, wouldn't that be the beginning of an interesting conversation?

A

January 5, 2021

A Buffet of Interpretations!

Remember when a former Quebec Prime minister commented that we didn't work as hard as Ontarians or Americans? It created such a stink and provoked such a backlash, that most, if not all, who agreed with him kept their mouths shut. Everybody, from radio commentators to business leaders, pooh-poohed the former politician, saying he didn't understand, that he wasn't respecting the people. Because we were, after all, the best!

Back in 2006, he was referring to our lack of productivity. But if one reads between the lines, he was really talking about our collective character, a demonstration of our independence, our right to believe in anything we want and stand firm against any common obligation to do something we don't like.

Pick and Choose!

Based on the last few weeks of increasing

Photo by Asiya Kiev on Unsplash

infections, it appears, once again, that we do not understand clear instructions, but we seem, instead, to interpret these demands as a series of behaviors to choose from, like in a buffet. 48% of us interpret directives as optional. You pick one directive, modify it according to your own understanding of what it really means for you, personally, from your point of view, and that's that. You're good to go!

In a way, I'm a little sad because it's going to take a long time before buffets come back in style. I loved them because I could pick and choose whatever me-wants, whatever me-thinks, whatever me-believes in and... whatever me-anything!

Now, the Premier, who is also part of our collective mind-set, will be forced to become a disciplinarian. He won't like doing that because he was born to respect the rights of others to the point of waiting until our health system nearly crashes under its own weight and inefficiency.

My, my!

A Mild Case of Discipline

What are we to become if we must subject ourselves to a mild case of discipline? Or worse, if we decided that the common good was worth a little respect for those on the frontlines caring for those who are about to die?

A

January 9, 2021

The Last Days at the White House

The last days at the White House in January 2021 and the Führerbunker on April 1945. An interesting comparison.

I like writing fiction interlaced with a bit of reality. I like fantasizing about what could be. I like fast cars and I also like BBQ chicken with hot sauce.

By the same token, I like to write about real stuff, for example, sociopaths and how they hurt people. They have invaded my consciousness since 2010 or thereabouts, because I worked with a few.

That said, my propensity to exaggerate to make a point has been forever put into its place by the last days of Trump's presidency. There's nothing that would have made me predict the insurrection. Even in my wildest dreams! And I know why. It's because I don't have enough imagination and I can't and will not place myself in a sociopath's mind.

So here we are, in the midst of a

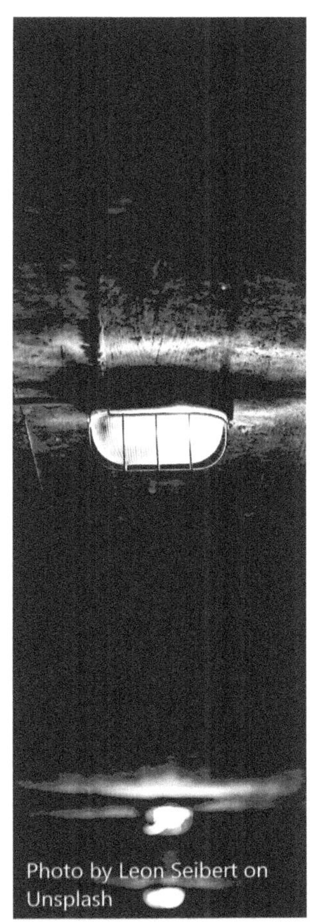

Photo by Leon Seibert on Unsplash

Faustian tale, looking south, baffled, mystified and confused, and I find myself asking how did more than 70 million people vote for a sociopath? Personally, I think they (sociopaths) should not be eligible for public office nor, if I had a say in it, for any leadership position.

What's strange, what amazes me, is how similar endings can occur more than seventy-five years apart: one in the White House and the other in the Führerbunker in Berlin.

For me, fiction will never be the same.

A

PS. I know what some of you are thinking about: probably the unimaginable. Well, stop that!

January 10, 2021

Rupert Murdoch

Current job: master architect of chaos, lies and Trump.

Australian-born American billionaire Rupert Murdoch owns, among other things, Fox News. Under his company News Corp, he created, with the help of Roger Ailes, Fox News. Ailes then proceeded to create the Donald Trump cult.

Let's not misread Murdoch's fundamental role in the Trump years: although the man is not a political animal, because he couldn't care less about Trump or anybody else, what really energizes him is the money his corporation makes off the US's political wars.

From what I can see with my own eyes, it appears that Murdoch doesn't really care what happens to the US while Trump's sociopathy is infecting the nation. He also doesn't care about what happens to ordinary Americans as a result of Trump's amazing mishandling of the pandemic.

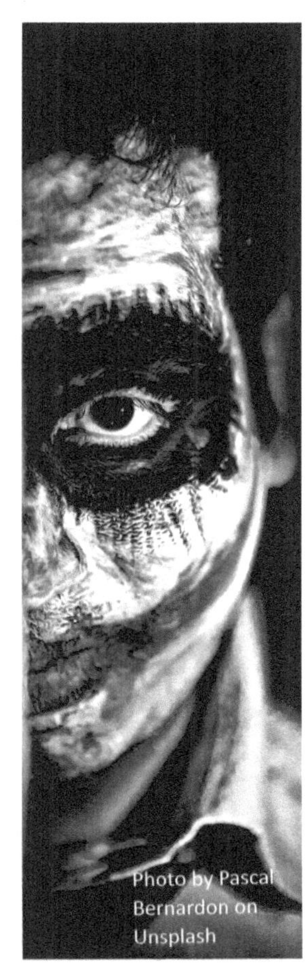

As I said, Murdoch only cares about Murdoch.

So, who is Rupert Murdoch?

He is the architect of the US's fall into a Trumpian abyss. Fox News, assisted by Trump's enablers, has become a degenerate instrument of blackmail, intimidation and sedition.

President-Elect Biden would be well served if Murdoch was sent packing to his native Australia; if, that is, the Aussies would take him back.

If Murdoch comes to your country, please, don't let him in. He's about as toxic as the Anti-Christ. He is the real Joker.

A

January 20, 2021

Inauguration of the New US President

Today, my life expectancy just got extended by 4 more years.

I watched, as many of you did, Joe Biden being sworn-in as the 46th U.S president. He called on Americans to end the "uncivil war".

I watched and I wept as the new President told his fellow Americans that he will defend the Republic.

The tears did not come from the pomp and pageantry of a swearing-in ceremony, neither did they come from songs and civil speeches or poetry.

I'm afraid it's much more personal.

I realized why I had tears. The mere thought of not having to hear Trump's words, or see his face's *Mussolinian** contempt, made me realize that I was now free.

I did not have to hold the remote control to change channels as soon as I perceived his face on my TV screen. My tears were a sign of my newfound freedom from his foulness, his vulgarities and his immoral obscenities of the

Photo by Jason Leung on Unsplash

past 4 long years. My soul told me that I was finally free from the Trash, the Rubbish, the Unclean, the Murky and the Perverted!

I was a free man again. I was also relieved because I could breathe again. I could now watch TV without the remote in my hands, always ready to change channels. I could now behave as a normal human being.

I think I feel much better. Happier. Healthier. Stronger.

I hope I will live longer than expected and prosper, with peace in my heart and with my sincere gratitude to the American people.

A

Mussolinian: expression derived from (Benito) Mussolini, an Italian politician who founded and led the National Fascist Party.

January 27, 2021

Greedy, Self-Centered and Treacherous

Would you believe me if I told you that there are greedy, self-centered and treacherous Canadians who are aggressively shipping our manufacturing potential abroad!

These incredibly destructive individuals boast that they can manufacture any product abroad (China...) and ship directly to customers around the world. What they don't say is they are sabotaging our economy, destroying our jobs and wiping out our country's autonomy... for their own pockets and outrageous homes.

Ask yourself why are we waiting for vaccines? Why aren't we first in line? Why did we have to wait for a pandemic for the government to think about building a vaccine manufacturing plant in Canada?

∞

Side 1 of the Answer: The Pain (Otherwise Known as the Pandemic)

Let's start off at the beginning. The vaccine is not the solution. It's part of the solution, yes, but not all of it. But let's be a bit more lucid about viruses. They existed 3.5 billion years before humans evolved on Earth. They're neither dead nor alive. Their genetic material is embedded in our own DNA, constituting close to 10% of the human genome.

So why, you may ask, is the vaccine against Covid-19 not the ultimate solution?

Well, that's a good question. Let me try my luck at explaining myself.

Basically, I don't believe for a minute that we, as a nation, will sooner or later come back to normal. There will be a number of waves due to mutations and that will continue until we can find a way of ridding ourselves of bad viruses. Those dangerous to humankind. But that won't happen in my lifetime, your lifetime, your children's lifetimes, etc. I fear that we will have to adapt and that means we will learn to live with the virus and its cousins, live with multiple vaccines, live with new drugs to reduce complications and yes, live with governments around the world who will continue to balance health and money -unsuccessfully.

∞

Side 2 of the Answer: Getting Back Our Autonomy as a Nation

Believe it or not, we have the skills to be in control of our destiny. To be able to make vaccines right here. If you haven't noticed lately, our nation is at the mercy of others because we have, over the years, exported our manufacturing capabilities abroad. We simply can't produce the vaccines we need now, anywhere in Canada, because we're not a manufacturing nation anymore. We're not manufacturing practically everything we need. Think of it as a gift from us to the rest of the world and, ironically, we're proud of it!

To be more precise, we were told and encouraged by governments, federal and provincial, over the last 30 years, to do business globally or we'd miss the boat. We have tons of French and English-speaking Canadian companies helping our businesses ship abroad their manufacturing for a very short-term gain. I was writing 20 years ago about how naïve it was to believe that giving our jobs away would help us develop better jobs here at home. Look at us now: we have become a site of low-paying jobs and one-, two- or three-dollar stores, sort of Mini-Banks or China outlets.

Now, our starved chickens are coming home to roost... meaning that the bad decisions we took in the past are coming back to bite us on our proverbial *derrieres.*

So, what to do?

Making Stuff Here in Our Country

I've been racking my brains about this, and I have come to the conclusion that we can't rely on governments to help us because making stuff here in our country is not a priority. What is needed is business acumen: the will to compete, to initiate, to innovate and to display a fair amount of courage that governments and their minions simply cannot ensure. Ask any politician who had a career in business and is now managing government policy, protocols and tons of paperwork, what he or she is doing to prioritize manufacturing in Canada?

I've tried to get people interested: to get a conversation going about being more autonomous as a nation. But it's not working. So, I've come back to square one: education, the bedrock of our civilisation. We need our underrated teachers and professors from across the country to bail us out, to ask the following question to all students from kindergarten kids to Ph.Ds., from professional and technical high school kids to military academy cadets:

"How Can We Produce This Here, Right in Our Own Backyard, and Make a Profit?"

We have to start with our young: open minds. Unlike us older folks, they will understand. We need to develop an army of entrepreneurs and manufacturers. We don't need a new learning module, or change the way we teach kids, or another reinvention of our educational system. No. We just need the right question to get them going in the right direction: "How can we produce this here, right in our own backyard and make a profit?"

We also need our own entrepreneurs, businesspeople from all corners of the country, to start doing their part and ask the following question to their bankers, their shareholders, stakeholders, customers and their own family members:

"How can we produce this here, right in our own backyard, and make a profit?"

Do we want to stop the bleeding of our culture and economic autonomy?

We can do this.

Just ask the question.

Ask it!

A

February 8, 2021

The Wake-up Call

When I think about it, it was the mother of all wake-up calls!

Fifteen years ago, well before the pandemic, our lives began to change. Louise's parents and brother, as well as my mother, started to rely more and more on us. Time was ticking toward ill-health and intensive care.

We had to take the lead. And so, we began parenting our two families. That meant that our lives were going to take a turn for the worst. Taking care of family members meant decisions and observations, fear and anxiety, which inevitably ended up in a near full time occupation for the two of us. If you don't understand what I'm describing, give it a little time, you will soon find out.

We also began to visit hospitals, emergency wards, doctors and specialist of all kinds, nurses, private nurses, support staff, admin staff, security personnel, technical staff, resident care staffers and God knows who else. During that time, our travels abroad were few and very short.

Photo by Sharon McCutcheon on Unsplash

Conclusions

15 years ago, as we began to visit hospitals on a regular basis, morning, noon and night, we witnessed dysfunctionality. Hospitals that could only be described as organizations devoid of clear hierarchies, of clear leadership, of real supervision and of basic accountability. We came to two conclusions:

1. Our health system was dysfunctional because... nobody was really in charge.
2. Someone very high up, wanted it that way because you can't become dysfunctional by accident!

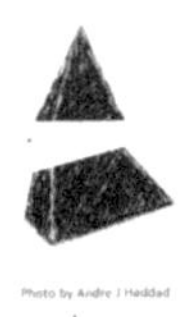

Photo by André J Haddad

Yes, it's that simple! No one person, at each level of those organizations, was in charge, in command, at the helm, giving orders, answerable to someone, accountable to make hard decisions.

Louise and I are both industrial psychologist and we believed back then that we had seen most if not all organizational issues. We had worked practically everywhere on this planet. Nevertheless, we had the mother of all wake-up calls.

Most all employees in the hospitals we visited were struggling to do their jobs, while others were trying very hard to do the least amount of work possible.

And nothing has changed, except for the pandemic, which now reveals our deep flaws, systemic weaknesses and incredible management failings.

∞

Sinking Ship!

I hear the drums telling us to pour more money in a ship that lacks captains and supervisors with authority and a real support system for employees. What I don't hear is an invitation for the nonperformers in management to work elsewhere.

But let's remember one thing: every problem starts at the top, the very top.

As a consultant, I always warned my clients that after reviewing their operations, I would comeback and tell them what they were doing wrong.

Most times it's obvious!

A

February 10, 2021

Why Did the First Wave Hit the Elderly?

I'll make my answer short and sweet based on what we lived through.

During a period of 10 years, Louise and I were responsible for our 2 families. We were in charge of parenting our parents. We made decisions. They moved into private, expensive facilities. We were on site, at their senior home, at least twice every week, if not more often. But while we were doing that, we saw things you might not like to hear.

Photo by André John Haddad

1. Few residents had visitors in both senior homes where our families lived. Maybe 10% got a visit from a family member every now and then.
2. If you didn't visit your parents on a regular basis, talked to the employees and management on a regular basis, your parents didn't get the attention they required or paid for.
3. They died because you weren't there. Your parents didn't need Covid-19 to kill them.

Here's my question to you:

Do we need an inquiry to find that out? Why Covid-19 hit the elderly and decimated them?

Here's my answer to you:

You bet we do. And you can count on us to be witnesses for the dead.

A

February 15, 2021

Mike Ward

I laugh when stand-up comics remind me of who we are as a people, the things we do and how we go about our lives. These comedians make us laugh at ourselves.

I don't laugh when stand-up comics ridicule individuals, people like you and me. As I said, I don't laugh because it's cheap comedy, callous, hurtful and cowardly. It's verbal aggression against a specific person in the name of free speech and money.

Take Mike Ward: according to his website site he is "... an award-winning bilingual comedian based out of Montreal, Canada...." His type of comedy is according to his website... "too dirty for traditional television..."

The comedian argues he had the right to mock disabled singer Jérémy Gabriel in 2010. His case is being reviewed by the Supreme Court. I don't know what the Justices are going to do with that. I trust them to make the right decision.

I'd like to believe that no right, including free speech, is absolute.

A

February 17, 2021

Time to Change Leaders in Ottawa

Solid, competent and well-organized political parties help guarantee that we, the people of Canada, don't fall into a Trumpian nightmare.

In fact, strong political parties, whether federal, provincial or municipal, require sound leadership, a healthy dose of honesty and the respect for the people and their future. The basic material or key building blocks of any political party are its values and party programs.

That guarantee rests on a party's history and steadfast focus on a better life for its citizens, not the worship of a leader. The Trumpian cult was built around a person's outrageous and offensive lies, a style better suited for a horror movie. Trump and Fox News were Rupert Murdoch's inventions and a ticket to the White House. The cult was nurtured to help a sociopath get elected. Trump's constant embellishments and the exaggerations -that a great many

Photo by Joy Real on Unsplash

Americans still believe, nearly caused the downfall of the US Republic.

Let's return to Canadian politics. The Trudeau cult was built around a person's name. A naïve belief that Justin Trudeau had enough substance to lead a country. I must admit, I believed he did. Well, I was wrong. He's certainly not his father. Intellectually, Justin Trudeau is a junior compared to his dad. He's proved it so many times, it hurts.

Like I said, we need good leaders and I'm sorry to say that the Federal Liberals are in trouble. They need to change the PM before the next election. We have a boy in power and he reveals himself as mostly incapable. He lacks judgement and courage, both characteristics impossible to teach or fake.

To all Liberal Federal MPs and party members: get your act together before someone else decides to do a job on your party. The best weapon the opposition parties possess at this point in time is our current Prime Minister. The longer he stays in power, the weaker we become as a democracy.

That's unacceptable.

Please do the right thing at the next Liberal National Convention.

A

February 19, 2021

What You Should Know about *Tout le monde en parle*

Radio Canada's version of *Tout le monde en parle* (or TLMEP) with Guy A. Lepage and Dany Turcotte, is a poor man's version of *Tout le monde en parle*, the French talk show broadcasted from Paris on France 2 from September 5, 1998 to July 8, 2006. It was hosted by Thierry Ardisson and produced by Catherine Barma. This French show was exciting not only because it dared being politically incorrect, but also because Ardisson was fearless, arrogant, feared, a womanizer, a *manizer* and a wit that touched on the genius.

TLMEP was adapted for Canadian TV. We settled on normals: Lepage and Turcotte were chosen to host the show. That was the first mistake. After the initial show, they should have cancelled the whole thing.

On the other hand, the original French show offered challenges and incredible entertainment. Ours was... simply lacking in everything but commercials.

Oh, yes. I forgot to mention that the Canadian taxpayer was TLMEP's major shareholder. The show brought the bar down when compared to the original French version. The only quality of our homegrown version was its superior capacity to simplify issues in order for a 2-year-old to better understand what the adults were babbling about. To say the show was superficial would be an overstatement. Or is that an understatement? I'm not too sure. Take your pick.

Our show has been playing for 17 long, long seasons.

I remember (and you should too) Lepage saying at the very beginning that we shouldn't criticize the show as taxpayers because our share would only come to 25 cents a show, which he said, he'd personally pay back to anyone asking for a refund.

Well, I'm asking.

Let's see here, that's 17 seasons, say 30 shows every year, multiplied by 25 cents, comes to a little over a hundred dollars.

Here's the good part: I promise to send the cheque to charity, Centraide, to be precise.

A

February 23, 2021

Made in Canada!

We're in trouble with China and we currently have no leverage to change things.

This post is not about Meng Wanzhou's arrest in Vancouver, about imprisoned Canadians in Chinese prisons, about China's genocide of the Uighur people or how the Chinese are blocking our canola exports. The subject matter is about Canada's weak, if not fictitious, capacity to retaliate in kind to China's bullying foreign policy. We Canadians simply do not have what it takes to force China to do... anything!

Please let me explain. It seems it's not very difficult to get in trouble with the Chinese. Not too long ago, we got in hot water with the Chinese because Parliament condemned the persecution and genocide of China's Uighurs and other Turkic Muslims in western Xinjiang region. All we had to do to get in real trouble was to

Photo by Andre John Haddad

135

say it's bad to kill people because of their race.

∞

China's 3 Step Retaliation Policy

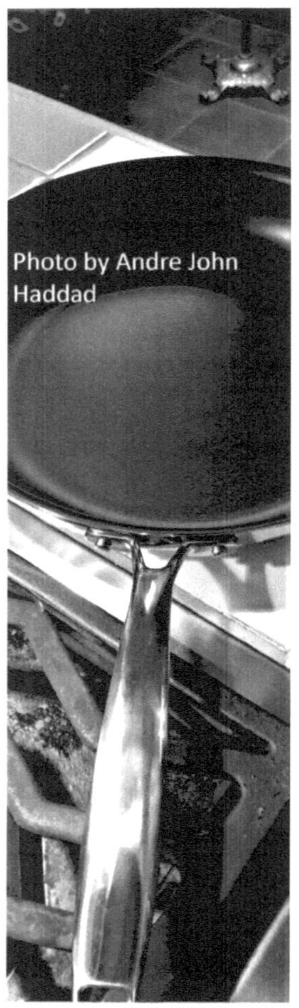

Like you, I'm aware that Canadians in China can be a problem these days because some of us have been arrested. This is what probably happened: first step, China does a Putin (i.e., invent an illegal act, arrest a Canadian, detain a Canadian, and sentence a Canadian to prison or to death). That's the first step.

Step two: China imposes sanctions, tariffs, breaks commercial ties, etc. These sanctions can cripple a part of our economy because, as I said so many times before, we don't manufacture any longer in Canada. We must import, and we do a lot of that with China.

Step three: China blackmails other countries to keep their mouths shut, tight. Otherwise, their own citizens could be persecuted for belonging to the wrong country and wind up in jail or on death row.

Fortunately, we aren't travelling to China these days because of the pandemic. However, and most importantly, China will continue to condemn fellow Canadians for being in the wrong place at the wrong time.

I can't tell you exactly how I feel about that because... let's just say that the language I would use to describe what I'm thinking would contain too many religious references.

One more thing about manufacturing.

I purchased a non-stick pan. Believe or not, it's made in... yes, wait for it, Canada. Personally, I'm fanatical about buying anything made over here rather than over there. Our sovereignty as a nation depends on it.

It's our only leverage.

A

February 25, 2021

Montreal Hockey: Mr. Marc Bergevin

It seems like the manager is... overwhelmed.

According to Wikipedia, Mr. Marc Bergevin is a Canadian professional ice hockey executive and former player. He is currently the general manager of the Montreal Canadiens of the National Hockey League. Hours after Canadiens' GM Marc Bergevin fired Claude Julien, the GM said the team needed a new voice.

Please let me be that new voice for just a moment.

When I told you a few months ago that I had a short talk with owner Geoff Molson, he confided that he had a pretty good team this year.

Okay, I believe him. But does he have the right management team?

Let's look at the Montreal Canadiens from a business point of view. After all, the team is, first and foremost, a business. As a management consultant, I always warn my clients that whatever happens, I'll come back and tell them what they are doing wrong or what they aren't doing.

In this case, it doesn't take an industrial psychologist to know that the Canadians fired the wrong person. The one at the top is always responsible for what happens in his organization. That's what I have observed over and over again, for the last 45 years. I heard his interview on 98.5 yesterday. I couldn't believe it. The team's GM has lost it. He almost said he had no idea what to do next.

If the owner would have asked me for my advice, I would have told him to change the lock on Bergevin's office door.

Mr. Bergevin needs to go. Now! Even though we're in the middle of the season. Yes, he's that bad.

A

March 6, 2021

I Was Thinking...

Uh-oh! What now?

Well, it just so happens that I was thinking about our shared behaviors during this pandemic. There are many conclusions we can come up with, but I'd like to concentrate on one. I call it Who-We-Are.

I think of the pandemic as a test for humankind, how we're coming together and finding ways to survive.

Photo by Jason Leung on Unsplash

As far as I can see, there are 3 clear results:

#1: 50% of people just want to get through it. They're scared.

#2: about 25% don't give a damn about anyone else but themselves.

#3: another 25% do everything they can to help.

When I think about it, I feel we're failing as a species to, as the song goes…, "Come Together".

After reading this, my *esposa* asked me, "Who are you? In which category do you think you fit?"

I said to myself, it's one thing to arrange the world into 3 categories, but it's quite another to admit where I fit. Okay, I get it. I need to put my cards on the table.

I think I fit in the first category: the 50% who just want to get through it in one piece.

To do that, my wife and I have a plan. We will get vaccinated as soon as we can. We will continue to follow the rules as best as we can. We are freely sacrificing some of our liberties to stay out of harm's way and keep others safe as well. We stay 2 meters away from others, always wearing a mask outside our home. We exercise or do something every day. We eat healthy foods. And we call friends to see how they're doing.

That said, I have to admit that I have this sinking feeling that I'm not doing enough.

But that's as far as I'll go, for now.

What about you?

A

March 9, 2021

Really Bad Decision by Parents

In fact, it was a wrong decision based on a wrong diagnostic and it took really bad judgement to make that happen.

This week, some parents decided to keep their young children at home rather than sending them off to school. The parents are protesting against the wearing of masks by young children, arguing the masks cause stress and harm.

Photo by Julien L on Unsplash

The parents' spokesperson added that she was troubled after reading thousands of messages from parents who worried about their children's development. She said the boycott would last another 2 days and if the government didn't back down, they would continue to protest.

∞

What's the Problem?

Here's the real issue: unless the child suffers from a cognitive or developmental problem, children can and do adapt to almost anything if we, as parents, provide the right context.

Children afraid of wearing masks take their cues from their mothers and fathers. If parents are worried, then the children will automatically feel the same way. This is what children do. They mimic, copy and learn.

I'm sorry to say it again: not all parents are adults. Some are still stuck in their adolescence. As a result, we have adolescents pretending to be adults while doing their best to raise their children.

Think about it: this cuing (prompting and signalling) behavior also happens with adults as they take their cues from their bosses, bankers, husbands, wives, friends, TV… and then they act accordingly.

If we change the cueing to our children, we change their behavior: from fearful to confident to happy.

So please, dear parents, look in the mirror and remind yourself that you are the reference, the guide and the model to copy.

It's all about you, mom and dad. Be confident and stop, for heaven's sake, bitching in front of your children, as if you knew everything.

A

March 28, 2021

Wake Up! It's Vaccine Day

Louise and I just got our first dose this morning. Didn't ask what brand of vaccine was running through our veins, but they told us, anyway. To be honest, as far as I'm concerned, the best vaccine is the one you get.

Unfortunately, at least half the world's population will have to wait to get their vaccine. Which makes it dangerous for the rest of us to rediscover our world. The bottom line is all about the numbers: the only safe world is one where everyone is vaccinated regardless of where they live.

One more thing: the vaccination center in St-Jerome was efficient, clean, and, let me say again, efficient, well-organized, competent, professional and courteous. Couldn't find anything to bitch about. Please don't worry about that last sentence. Give me a few minutes and I'll think of something...

A

PS. The third wave has begun. Shouldn't surprise anyone: self-discipline is not our

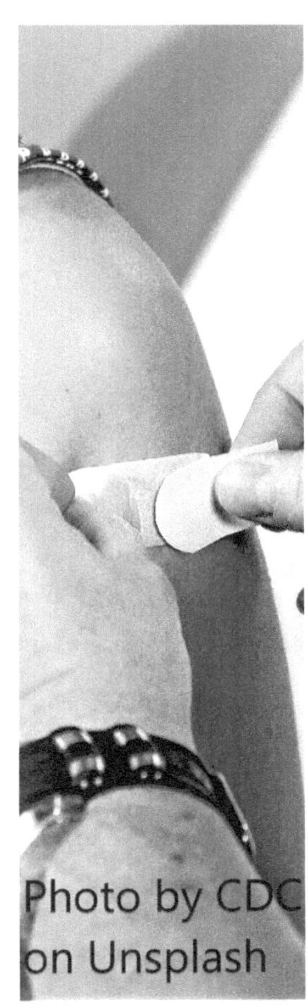

strong suit. For that reason, the fourth wave will happen as summer takes hold of our lives once again. Which means more people will die because some of us don't give a damn about the lives of others.

PS. As for the non-believers who think that Covid is nothing more than the flu, what can I say: they have been making bad decisions all their lives and will continue to do so until they die. Please remember that their incredible lack of judgement can't be fixed. God bless them anyway, for even idiots are welcomed in heaven.

April 4, 2021

I Wish You a Happy Easter, Mr. Legault

And thank you for your leadership, your devotion to the people you represent and, most of all, thank you for being a caring human being. But there's more to you than what you choose to admit to yourself or others.

I see a person who's clearly imperfect as are we all. A person who's learning in a very personal way that life is precious and that, as Prime Minister, you can't save everyone. A person who has to deal with new information that has direct repercussions on the lives and deaths of millions of people. A person who makes decisions that would normally break any man or woman's heart. A person

Photo by Priscilla Du Preez on Unsplash

who now recognizes the true nature of the virus, has an idea of what is coming up and who does not know if the people will be able to handle new challenges ahead of us, here in Quebec and the rest of the world.

In that context, I sincerely wish you'd take better care of

yourself. When I saw you last week on the news, I told my wife that you were aging prematurely. I know you didn't think your time in office would be caught up in malady, fear and every kind of contradictions a man could handle in one day. Nevertheless, your life after Covid will depend on how well you take care of yourself today and tomorrow.

I've seen it before. I'm sorry, but I have to be clear. I hope I am now. Take care of yourself. Sacrifice and devotion to your people have a heavy price tag, especially when not considering our own wellbeing.

Again, Happy Easter, Mr. Prime Minister.

A

April 25, 2021

Deep Down the American Psyche

We all have our own individual personalities, but Derek Chauvin's case is really about something else altogether. It's about what's underneath a people's psyche. Its foundations and footing. *Derek Michael Chauvin is a former police officer who was convicted of the murder of George Floyd while on duty.*

∞

What's This All About?

What I found was disturbing: I call it a primeval survival instinct. A large group of Americans share this instinct and, as we all witnessed in the last presidential election, it's tearing them apart.

No, I'm not talking about racism. That would be too easy and spectacularly naïve. Calling the culprit (Derek Chauvin) racist would also prevent us from truly

understanding what's really going on.

Fact is, the US will become a minority white nation by 2045. In your lifetime. That is essentially what's scaring the living daylights of most white American Republicans and some Democrats!

Putting myself in the shoes of an average American Republican, I began to think that the only way for whites to stop the foreseeable US demographic trends, would be to borrow from Hitler's workbook and start a sociological holocaust which would probably end the existence of the US republic as we know it.

Sociological Phenomenon

Whether a sociological phenomenon or deep programming at the cellular level, my conclusions are the same. It's about the fear of losing dominance: an instinct that keeps some Americans awake at night. Dominance over the country's electoral college or anything that's linked to white ascendancy. One more thing: there is also the fear of being treated like a minority. The irony of *"What goes around comes around,"* is simply dizzying!

I've been pondering for years about the ramifications of a white minority. I'm convinced, now more than ever, that the latest incarnation of the Republican Party is sensing its own demise at the hands of mothers of different color.

I feel racism has been Act 1 of an old, active, aggressive and rebellious strategy against the racial demographics that are, as we speak, reshaping America, before our eyes.

The folly is to think that heavyweight demographic trends can be stopped.

Now, that's naïve.

A

May 4, 2021

Another Useless Government Report

It's not going to help anyone.

The Laurent Commission Report on creating a caring society for our children and youth finally produced its findings. The Special Commission was created in the wake of the murder of a seven-year-old child in Granby in April 2019.

In a nutshell, I'm not impressed. Here's why.

As anyone leading an organization will tell you, the easy part

in management is coming up with recommendations. Lots and lots of good, needed and strategic advice. That said, the Laurent Report does not really impress me because it doesn't take a Commission to come up with ideas. The world is full of good ideas and proven practices on how to make sure children grow up to become happy, healthy and competent adults.

The whole point of most Commissions is to discover opportunities to perfect, enhance and finally recommend. That's usually where a Commission's responsibility ends. Again, that's the easy part. The hard part, the critical element, is its implementation.

∞

Execution

Organizations succeed or fail on the execution of plans. This is where most Commissions fail because they usually don't know the first thing about how organizations work or change. Moreover, strategies most often fail because they aren't well executed.

J Dimon, CEO of JPMorgan Chase, is credited with saying "I'd rather have a first-rate execution and second-rate strategy any time than a brilliant idea and mediocre management."

The lesson here is that anyone can come up with a set of good recommendations. Finding the right person to execute those recommendations should have been the most important part of the Laurent Commission. It should have been about finding a leader with the authority to make the changes, a person with high management skills, an individual with a deep understanding of how organizations work, with a powerful vision to share with employees and a strong will to succeed... all in the name of our children.

The DPJ's* leader should have been the beginning and the end of all the Commission's findings. He or she is the culture, the change maker, the person who will instill a new vision and the associated behaviors required.

I have a very bad feeling about what's going to happen in the future because we will fail (again) to find the right person (with the authority) to do the job. We will fail because we will be fearful of naming a person who will disturb, interrupt and dictate a new way of doing things. Contrary to popular opinion, we hate those who make the changes. Fundamentally, we are afraid of not being pertinent and competent in light of the changes made in the organization.

Let me be clear about what we have learned about organizations and change: Karl Moore's work entitled "Strategy without Execution is Hallucination!" says it all.

Hallucination, indeed.

A

* The DPJ (Direction de la protection de la jeunesse / Youth protection): a provincial organization that receives reports about children who may be in need of protection. The organization assesses these children's life conditions and makes decisions to ensure their protection. It also wants to guarantee that the interests of these children are protected in accordance with their rights.

May 10, 2021

Obsessively Clean!

My very best friend just got himself installed a Carrier Ultraviolet (UV) Germicidal Lamp System for his home. Isn't that a mouthful?

Carrier claims that mold and mildew can impact our indoor air quality if they build up inside our HVAC (Heating, Ventilation, and Air Conditioning) system's indoor cooling coil. Carrier's system prevents bacteria from becoming airborne.

I think my very best friend is going a bit overboard. I mean, what next? A portable UV lamp attached to our body?

Well, I'm not one to judge. It's his life and he's allowed to do anything he wants. Right?

All I can say is that the installation was done at 1h pm yesterday, and I must admit, I'm breathing cleaner air already!

A

Photo by Serge Kutuzov on Unsplash

May 13, 2021

Anxious Children!

According to researchers, Quebec adults are anxious and display signs of depression during the pandemic. One adult out of five exhibits symptoms linked to anxiety or depression. The pandemic has also seriously weakened the mental health of young people in high school, college and university. Nearly half of them (48%) show disturbing traces of anxiety or depression. At this point in time, there is no reason to believe that these survey results don't apply to the Canadian population as a whole.

Upon reading these results, I find myself incapable of feeling empathy, sympathy or compassion. Strange as it may seem, I feel somewhat angry that we, as a nation, have fathered a generation of fragile individuals, incapable of finding a way to succeed in the midst of adversity.

Two thoughts come to mind: the lack of resilience of those seriously affected by the pandemic, as well as some guilt on my

Photo by Alliance Football Club on Unsplash

part for not being more compassionate towards them. That said, I'm clearly not impressed by surveys and commentators who declare "ad nauseam" that 20% of the population is in need of psychological assistance.

One, I don't trust surveys because in the last 30 years, I found that people lie. When do we lie, you ask? That's not a difficult question to answer: we lie all the time. We lie to mom and dad, brothers and sisters, spouses, friends, teachers and to ourselves. But we especially lie on surveys.

Two, it appears that 20% of us are suffering. Which means that they are not coping with what the pandemic is dishing out. I'm not talking about lack of food, shelter or clothing. No one's being shot in the streets, no armored tanks are destroying neighborhoods, no military jets are bombing our streets, no rockets are blasting away any remnants of civil society.

No. Our friends and neighbors are suffering because they can't see their friends, visit their favorite coffeeshop and bar, go dancing, attend school or place of work.

I know for a fact that some find the pandemic hard and cruel. They do because they have not learned to become resilient*. I'm afraid they were raised to live in an idealistic world where everything they want is there for the taking.

As most Canadians will tell you, life can be a bitch and one must learn to succeed in a difficult world filled with promise and disappointment. Ups and downs. Wars and Olympics. The pandemic we're going through is just another of Mother Nature's creatures. No more, no less.

If you're thinking of having children, think about what life is really about and prepare your kids to deal with adversity and boredom, difficulty and hard times, as well as the incredible beauty of how humans bounce back and thrive, and love, and succeed.

A

*According to the Merriam-Webster dictionary, resilience is a strength that certain men and women possess. A sturdy refusal to acknowledge defeat, which aids them as effectively in affairs of the heart as in encounters of a harsher and more practical kind. The word resilience derives from the present participle of the Latin verb *"resilire"*, meaning "to jump back" or "to recoil."

May 18, 2021

The Birthday Gift That Did Not Keep On Giving!

It was wrapped in the most beautiful ruby red paper. The bow was exquisite.

The present was encased in a special container with a black velvet lining. But she wasn't there yet. Herself was still looking at the box and wondering what could be so precious that I had taken the trouble to gift wrap it so stylishly.

What did you do again? she asked me. She knew I could go overboard, and of course I had. She was, after all, already the love of my life, though 

thinking back, I think I love her infinitely more today than I did then, 50 years ago.

Back to my story. I was too happy to answer her question. Perhaps too nervous, anxious or scared she wouldn't like what I got her. I discovered early in life that I always loved giving rather than receiving. That way, I never got disappointed. Still true to this day, but there's a wrinkle. A month ago, she bought the fourth Beast, just because it makes me happy. As far as she's concerned, a car is transportation. She couldn't care less whether she was driving a Ford, or heaven forbid, a Mazda. So no, I'm never ever disappointed anymore. I drive a Beast. What else can a man ask for!

Again, forgive me. Back to my story.

We're all sitting on the floor. The apartment, no bigger than my garage, was all Louise's friend could afford. The good thing was it wasn't too far from the university. We had just begun our third-year psychology and we were studying very hard. I also had a job as a barman at the Dorval Hilton, so I could splurge once in a while.

Should I open it now? she asked.

Yes, yes, everyone said in unison. We were the Brat Pack. We did everything together and any excuse was good for a party.

Come on, I said. It's just paper.

She carefully peeled off the wrapping paper. And there it was.

Créations Lucas Jewellery Designer, printed in 3D for all to see.

The box was way too big for a bracelet or a ring. Herself looked at me suspiciously. What's going on, she said. I could tell I had her attention. Everyone was mystified.

Go on, I said. It's your birthday gift. Go on!

Herself opened the box and at that moment I had proof that I was right. She loved them. Both of them. I could tell because she was crying.

I was smiling from ear to ear. She, on the other hand, was still crying.

"I knew you would love them, but..." I said.

She turned to me and said, "...Ah! Thank you...!" She put the box down and rushed out of the room.

I was stunned. Then her best friend came to me and said, "What were you thinking. This is her birthday... And you give her ashtrays! Two of them! Ashtrays, really?"

She also walked away, angry as hell.

That day stayed with me for a long time. I had learned something important. No good will come from ashtrays, or anything I would like to receive as a gift. It's all about what she dreams about, what she secretly craves for. I swore to myself that I would never make that mistake again.

No, more, ashtrays!

Thirty Years Later

Herself and I were on a city tour which included a few Berlin Museums. We were told that the Museum we were visiting was one of a kind: they collect, preserve, display and investigate modern and contemporary art, we were told by our guide.

As we were walking by another display, I slammed on the brakes.

"Louise! Louise!" I said, loud enough for everyone to hear. "Look! Your ashtrays."

I pointed to a display of what was called Contemporary and Inspired: Form and Beauty.

Herself looked at me.

"Well, what do you know?" She said, and then turned around as if nothing happened.

Lesson two: it doesn't matter if the damn ashtrays had been displayed at the Louvre. It wouldn't have made any difference. Not one iota. An ashtray's an ashtray's an ashtray!

I hope you know what I'm talking about, because if you don't, you're in deep trouble!

A

June 1, 2021

What's New on the Hockey Scene?

A feeling of joy resulting from Toronto's misfortune!

Is that even possible?

It's called *schadenfreude*. It's German, and it's made up of two words: *Schaden*, which means harm or damage, and *Freude*, which means joy. *Schadenfreude* is a complex emotion where, rather than feel sympathy, one takes pleasure from watching someone's misfortune.

And yep, it's real, it's human, it's... dare I say it, normal!

∞

Almost Ashamed

Surprisingly, I can't help myself. I'm almost ashamed... but happy at the same time. But how is this possible? A pleasure derived from another person's bad luck shouldn't be satisfying or funny. Right?

Photo by Heshan Chamikara on Unsplash

I don't know, but in this case, Montreal beating Toronto, at hockey, in Montreal, in front of 2,500 fans, is a gift from hockey heaven. Which really means that He is on our side and not theirs!

I know it's not fair. God should be unbiased and love every living creature in the universe, but Montreal beating Toronto was probably too much, even for Him.

That doesn't mean we'll win the Stanley Cup... Still, we can enjoy the pleasure of winning and the other guy's grief, if just for a couple of days.

So, enjoy and rejoice while you can, oh Montreal fans.

A

To be perfectly honest, I must remind you again that I feel a little guilty about the whole *Schadenfreude* stuff. Call it a... guilty pleasure. That said, we did win. Against all odds! In the middle of a pandemic. So, permit me to enjoy Toronto's shameful defeat at the hands of our glorious team.

Long live the Habs!

June 15, 2021

Organizational Culture: A Friendly Reminder

"We will need to change the organization's culture!" For your information, that's pretend science, and it hides a secret that no one wants to hear.

When you hear a politician, a TV or radio broadcaster, a senior manager, a union rep, a journalist, a judge, an HR manager, a change management expert, a consultant, a high-ranking government employee, anyone... start a sentence with "the culture of the organization must change...", remember just one thing: there is no such thing as an organizational culture.

I'm sure you've read or heard the following:

1. "Now's the time for the military to implement important changes to its culture."
2. "While welcoming the recommendations, we insist on the importance of a culture change at the DPJ (Quebec's Youth Protection

Agency).”
3. “Many of the problems faced by our company are attributed to its culture.”

Origin

The term organizational culture was introduced in the 1950s (Psychology Press Reissue, 2001) by Dr. Elliott Jaques, a Canadian psychoanalyst, in his book *The Changing Culture of a Factory*. Jaques defines organizational culture as common wishes, desires and aspirations and a commitment by employees to work together. In the 70ies, Industrial psychologists like myself were trained to deal with an organization's culture through change management strategies. I can clearly remember preaching the culture concept and predictably, I saw culture problems everywhere!

Happily, over time, I finally matured from blind apostle to adult observer, and I started to doubt the existence of an organization's culture. I searched for this culture-thing for years. Not surprisingly, I couldn't find it anywhere, except in the boss' office. Today, it's clear that the culture concept is counterfeit. There is no such beast because the so-called concept lives entirely in the boss' head. Most organizations have bosses and they lead through a version of a management structure: a boss more or less supervising employees. That's it. What we believe is a culture problem is in fact, the manifestation of a leader's personality, behaviors, words and decisions.

Let's change the vocabulary and see if it makes sense to you:
1. “Now's the time for the military to implement deep changes to its *leadership*.”
2. “While welcoming the recommendations, we insist on the importance of *changing the management staff* of the DPJ (Quebec's Youth Protection Agency).”
3. “Many of the problems faced by our company are attributed

to its *president and senior management.*"
I'll bet you don't hear that too often.

What Does the Culture Concept Really Hide?

Simply put, it conceals the fact that we keep leaders in their jobs, regardless of their performance. What we call culture is a mosaic of the leader's fundamental beliefs embedded in his or her personality, expressed through his or her expectations. Leaders are responsible, through their words, actions and decisions, to ensure an organization's continued existence.

The standard belief is that culture change takes 2-3 years to occur. Truth is, changing a leader and a company's performance can take from 1 week to 2 months, tops. The change required to succeed is simple and staring at us: new leadership. To make change happen, remember these 3 steps:

1. Change the leader.
2. Communicate the new leader's expectations.
3. Listen to employees on how best to implement the leader's plans.

When we keep the same management staff in place, or change a weak leader with a weak replacement, we usually get the same results. Weak leadership leads to no real change or improvements. Changing the culture entails spending a lot of money for nothing, which eventually leads to failure.

Closing

When you hear this sentence: "the culture of the organization must change…", remember, there is no such thing as an organizational culture. It's all smoke and mirrors.

The direction every employee follows almost to the letter is based on what the boss wants, how he or she wants it, when he or she wants it, and the consequences that follow.

Why Hide the Truth?

Because it's a lot safer to blame culture than to point fingers at the real culprits, i.e., top management! It's always management. There are no other reasons why an organization succeeds or fails: management, management, management and again, management!

A

June 27, 2021

Heading up North in the Middle of the Great Flood

It was 9h30 pm. I was driving up north. The first few minutes were uneventful. Business as usual. But then, as we gained access to Autoroute 15 North, that's the freeway between Montreal and the Laurentians, we encountered a little rain.

So far, so good, I said to myself. Driving in the rain is my specialty. I'm used to it, I'm good at it, even if Herself believes she's a better driver than I am. Again, business as usual, that is... until the wind started to push the car one way and the other.

Again, nothing to worry about. We were driving below the unofficial speed limit, which is in itself a bit strange. Please let me explain. Officially, the speed limit on the freeway is 100 kilometres an hour. The *Sureté du Quebec* (the state police), tolerates 119 kilometres an hour. Yes, they do have that power. If one's caught driving over 119, your ticket will register the number of kilometers over the official speed

limit that starts at 100 kilometers an hour. Now, that's fair. Right?

But I digress.

Suddenly, out of nowhere, the dark blue skies over the city of Laval turned ink black, followed immediately by the Great Flood.

Traffic crawled to 30 kilometer an hour. Some activated their flashers. We all ended up trying to avoid the famous road-gutters (2) found in each lane of the highway. Those were created by heavyweight trucks during our hot summers. These road gutters have been getting deeper and deeper to the point of causing a small jolt when changing lanes in dry weather.

Again, I can deal with that because the gutter thing is a minor issue, less than 2 inches deep. However, add torrential rains, winds, and driving the Autoroute suddenly turns into a summer sport of car-surfing while praying to God that we'll reach home in one piece. It felt like I was driving through a carwash gone haywire.

Not to Worry

Herself was commenting on how dangerous the road must be. I told her not to worry, that everything was under control. To be honest, I lied about that and continued to lie until we reached home an hour later. The so-call road gutters are the product of our Quebec Transport Department's lack of responsibility and professionalism. You should know that the Department is responsible for all provincial highways and their maintenance.

We are dealing with gross mismanagement. Over the last fifty years, I've been driving here and around the world and I can honestly say that our roads are way below world standards; some are dangerous while others don't have the right to call themselves roads or highways.

Regardless of who's in power in government, our roads remain bad, really bad, *"badder"* than bad. They are unsafe.

Let me be clear: Transport Department employees are not

responsible. They're just following orders. That's what you should remember. The real culprits are and have been, the Department's management staff as well as the different Transport Ministers over the years.

This can be fixed in 3 steps:

1. Change the management
2. Communicate the new leader's expectations
3. Listen to employees on how best to implement the leader's plans

Last night was by far the worst driving experience I've had the misfortune to live through.

A

July 7, 2021

Another Murder in La Perle des Antilles!

President Jovenel Moïse died in his private residence on the outskirts of the capital, Port-au-Prince. His residence was attacked by a group of armed mercenaries. His wife was also shot.

What's really happening in Haiti and, more importantly, why is it getting worse? Those are two important questions. Let me try to explain the situation for those who perhaps aren't aware of what's going on down there.

What No One Talks about in Public: A Corrupt Mind-set and a Greedy Outlook on Life

The fabulous grey-white dwellings perched atop the mountainside of Pétionville overlook Port-au-Prince. The scene from this vantage point is spectacular. It appears dreamlike

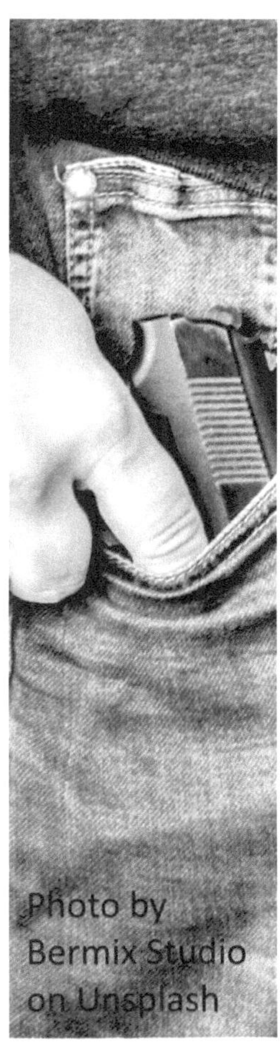

Photo by Bermix Studio on Unsplash

under the Haitian moonlight. Suspended in midair, the night fog provides the upscale village of Pétionville with an eerie and ghostly appearance, especially at night when all the imperfections of city life melt into the shadows. But foreign workers, consultants, international relief personnel, Development Bank officials, foreign police and military, all know better. The night hides and lies.

It's called a city because there's a lot of people living in one spot, cramped in spaces unfit for human beings, but that's a cruel and incomplete statement about the nature of Port-au-Prince. The Capital of Haiti is indeed a real city populated by the most courageous and resourceful people I have ever met anywhere, anytime. Ordinary people, running around the city trying to make a living, if you can call it living, are the good guys. If there's a heaven, I'm sure the best places are reserved for them.

Port-au-Prince has seen better times, but today calling it a capital is like calling Detroit delightful. Once you set foot in Port-au-Prince, you discover the true meaning of hell on earth.

Port-au-Prince is the capital of consultants. Experts from all over the world come to the capital to investigate and recommend what should be done with the country. They churn out reports that could fill a library.

Delegations from around the world, as well as their consultants, have been and still are the engines that keep some hotels and fancy bistros running. They are everywhere. Nations who want to help Haiti out of its misery will send consultants to Haiti to fact-find and report back. Development Banks, such as the World Bank, will also send consultants to either initiate a project or check up on a project's progress.

If I had to make a big, broad, nasty statement about what consultants have achieved over the years, I would have to say they've been a colossal waste of time and money. Very little of the money allocated to Haiti goes to its people. I should know, I was one of those consultants. In that capacity, I witnessed the following:

∞

Findings

The great majority of Haitians live in unbelievable poverty and danger because they have been governed by a greedy, racist, self-centered elite since the 1800. The Haitian *crème de la crème* has run its own people into the ground by making sure the rich Haitian families manage and control everything that has value in the tiny island state.

You'll see them in homes that defy the imagination atop Pétionville, in restaurants and bistros that compete with any fine dining establishment anywhere. You'll hear them reciting poetry in Paris. You'll see them driving the best and most expensive cars and SUVs in Haiti and Miami. They have drivers, cooks, maids, nannies and servants. You'll immediately recognise them.

For the poor, there's practically nothing left to do but a daily grind to make a few coins for supper and for a lousy tin roof over their heads. More to the point, one meal or one night's stay in one of Haiti's fine hotels could feed a family for a few months, perhaps more.

Again, I know this because, as I told you, I'm a consultant. I was there. Often. I was naïve. I thought I could do some good over there. I was terribly wrong.

A

PS. If I were mean and cruel, I'd tell you to go see for yourself. But that would not be the Christian thing to do, because... it's too dangerous.

July 11, 2021

Vladimir Vladimirovich Putin

Can Canadians ignore Vladimir Putin?
Should you?
This is his bio:
Vladimir Vladimirovich Putin, born 7 October 1952
Current employment: President of Russia
Net worth: $200 billion (2018)
Contact number: 8 800 200 23 16
Email: president@gov.ru

In April 2014, Putin annexed the eastern Ukraine's Donetsk and Luhansk regions. Russia's top politician in point of fact declared war on a sovereign nation.

In July 2021, Putin decided that Russia's sparkling wine was to be called Champagne from now on. Russia's top politician declared war on international commerce and its rules.

The list goes on, from murdering enemies, imprisoning dissenters, quashing opposition, disrupting democracies to supporting some of the world's worst dictatorships.

∞

Photo by Don Fontijn on Unsplash

So, Who Is Putin?

First off, it's clear that President Putin is a man who believes he can do anything he wants. He also believes everyone will let him do whatever he wants because he's the man with the big stick. The same man who has his finger on 6,800 nuclear weapons. That's a very big stick. It's enough bombs to literally split the planet in half.

Of the 144 million Russian citizens, he believes only he can restore Russia to its former glory. So, he plans to change the Russian constitution to allow him to stay in power until 2036. If that happens, he would be 84 years old by 2036. He is currently due to step down in 2024.

Secondly, to do and to think all of the above, we can easily come to the conclusion that Vladimir Vladimirovich Putin is a narcissistic individual, and, I believe, a true sociopath.

As a writer, I wrote about sociopaths in my books and articles. I've worked for them and with them. Whether we know it or not, sociopaths are in our lives. Like Putin, they create confusion. They lie. They hurt people. They can be found everywhere: in government and politics, business, education, law, religion, finance, in our own families... And they are close to us. Some, like Putin, can be highly visible, while others are more discreet. What they all have in common is their lack of conscience or remorse. While we can predict that encounters with sociopaths will usually end badly, there is nothing predictable about their choice of targets.

If that doesn't attract your attention, think of this:

Being a sociopath is for life. It's a condition, a disorder, an ailment or an illness. Some will say they are simply mentally ill. That would be a correct statement. It is, in fact, a mental illness. However, saying that doesn't mean you should run to help them. Professionals call this illness the antisocial personality disorder. Look it up. It's not a problem that can be fixed. It's permanent.

How can we say without the shadow of a doubt that Vladimir Vladimirovich Putin is a sociopath?

The illness' key characteristic is a persistent and a pervasive pattern of behaviors that violates or disregards the rights of others. It can be observed early in childhood, in adolescence and more consistently during adulthood.

Political organizations may recruit sociopaths for their top jobs because, basically, pushing folks around doesn't bother them. Sociopaths like to make people squeal and do as they are told.

If a sociopath is bad news, then a narcissistic sociopath with his finger on an atomic switch is a puppy on steroids. Which means that powerful narcissistic sociopaths can and will display behaviors that involve the following destructive patterns:

1. Callous disregard for the rights of others as well as unethical and antisocial reflexes
2. Deception and manipulation
3. Irresponsibility
4. Impulsivity and poor to no self-control
5. Lack of empathy, lack of guilt, lack of remorse
6. Sexual promiscuity
7. Shallowness
8. Indulging in self-praise and self-aggrandisement
9. Committing serious crimes

Takeaway

Never underestimate what Vladimir Putin is capable of doing in the future. Learn to understand who he really is. In the end, having the leader of a nuclear nation who believes he can do anything he wants is not only a bad idea, but a future filled with risk.

I know I'm repeating myself. I apologize for that. Nevertheless, let me say it one more time just to make sure we're on the same page: when you accept that Putin is a sociopath, it means that your brain will not allow you to circumvent the bitter truth any longer, because denying the risks Putin brings to everyone of us is naïve and self destructive.

∞

So What?

We need our leaders here to be brave. Brave enough to be aware of the damage the political sociopaths can do to people's way of life… and as much as this is painful to say, courage is indeed required.

However, with our current leadership in Ottawa, how well are we positioned to stand up to such people?

As I said, our nation requires brave, bold and intelligent politicians.

I guess we need to work on that, don't we?

A

July 16, 2021

Hemingway

Want to read one of the best novels ever written?

After viewing Ken Burns and Lynn Novick's three-part, six-hour documentary series, "Hemingway", I decided to read one of his works. I felt I had to. Even though I was educated in French and consequently Hemmingway was never on my list of must-read-books, I felt I had to read him, to understand the man and the author. I had no choice. I was motivated.

Three weeks later, I got hold of most of his works and I chose *For Whom the Bell Tolls*. I picked that particular novel because some said it was a masterpiece. It was published in 1940 and it tells a story set during the Spanish Civil War.

My research tells me that the Spanish Civil War was fought between 1936 and 1939. According to Claude Bowers, U.S. ambassador to Spain during the war, it was the "dress rehearsal" for World War II. About 200,000

men, women and children died from systematic murders, mob violence and torture. As you probably know, the winner, dictator Francisco Franco Bahamonde, governed Spain with an iron fist from 1936 until his death in November 1975. Historians tell us that El Caudillo or the Leader, believed he could turn Spain into a totalitarian state like Nazi Germany and Fascist Italy. Unfortunately, Franco achieved his goal. I'm amazed he stayed in power long after World War II ended. I'm also astonished he wasn't prosecuted for crimes against humanity while alive. But I digress.

For Whom the Bell Tolls tells the story of Robert Jordan, a young American volunteer attached to a Republican guerrilla unit during the war. As a dynamiter, he was assigned to blow up a bridge during an attack on the Spanish city of Segovia.

The title of Hemmingway's book comes from a sermon by the English writer and Anglican cleric John Donne. Born in 1572, he wrote a sermon containing the famous words "No man is an island, entire of itself; every man is a piece of the continent, a part of the main... any man's death diminishes me, because I am involved in mankind, and therefore never send to know for whom the bells tolls; it tolls for thee." That extraordinary sentence was written 400 years ago.

On October 18, 1940, literature critic Clifton Fadiman believed the work was a masterpiece.

Amid all the praise I heard about Hemmingway's writing, reading *For Whom the Bell Tolls* was nevertheless a disappointment, I felt a sadness I couldn't understand. But how can I say this without sounding foolish?

On November 5, 2019, BBC News listed *For Whom the Bell Tolls* on its list of the 100 most influential novels in history.

Who am I to contradict BBC News? I asked myself.

I don't know the answer to that. I'm just a reader. I love reading and writing.

I will admit, however, that I will read more of Hemmingway's works, because, just maybe, I wasn't thinking straight when reading *For Whom the Bell Tolls.*

Then again, maybe I was indeed thinking straight, and the author isn't as potent or relevant today as he was 80 years ago.

I honestly don't know what to think. I'm disappointed that I'm disappointed. I'll probably be put on trial for cultural heresy and sentenced to read Donald Trump's new one page book entitled *Look at me! I'm the best President in the whole history of history!*

Just kidding. Still, I don't know what to think.

Anyone out there can help me out? What am I missing? Didn't Ken Burns' three-part, six-hour documentary series on PBS explain it all?

A

July 23, 2021

Speak White!

Two words; a slur; a shove; a jab; an awakening!

Writer and playwright Michèle Lalonde died Thursday in Montreal. The author's legacy to culture remains to this day an important message about respect and common decency. Unbeknownst to me, her famous poem entitled "Speak White", written in 1968, had a lifelong impact on me.

How and why did that poem change me into what I've become?

∞

A&W

59 years ago, my mom dropped me off at the Dollard-des-Ormeaux's A&W. It was my first day, my first job, and I was pretty nervous. I didn't know what to expect.

Photo by David Lusvardi

My first assignment was to take customers' orders. In those days, a customer would order from his or her car. It was a true drive-in. That was done through a double-sided order station between parked cars. The intercom was how I got to hear customers. Customers would look at the menu, decide what they wanted, push the intercom button and place an order. When the order was ready, carhops would bring it out to customers' cars. They would ask the driver to roll up the window just a few inches so they (carhops) could snap on the tray with food and drinks.

∞

My First Customer Order

I honestly don't remember what the customer ordered, but I'd bet it was burgers, fries and A&W's famous Root Beer.

My job was to take down the order and tell the kitchen staff what the customer ordered, followed by a slip of paper which contained the order and number of the intercom.

When I had completed my first ever transaction with a real-life customer, I had my first real life experience as a member of the workforce.

A loud voice screaming at me from the kitchen said, if you want to work here, speak white, or else! You got that?

I looked at him. He was tall, about 20 years old, and looked really mean. I remember because he had really bad skin!

I was scared not only because someone was screaming at me but also because I didn't understand what the hell he was talking about. What does speak white mean? I must have looked confused because the manager came to my work station and said, listen kid (I was 14 years old), when you're speaking to the kitchen staff, give them the order in English. OK?

But the order was given to me in French, I said nervously, I just thought the...

No matter, the manager said. Just speak English and everything is going to be fine.

That night, I told my mom I didn't want to work there anymore. I told her what happened and she agreed that I was done with A&W.

The next summer, I started working at the Dorval Hilton. Whatever happened at the A&W didn't happen anymore because I had decided that no one would ever speak to me like that again.

I worked at the Hilton for more than 14 years in a variety of summer jobs as a bus-boy, barman and waiter. I learned to get by, how to get things done, how to get respect. I got some, but that came with a price. That said, no one ever told me to speak white again.

Needless to say, I never forgot my one-day job at A&W, the two words spoken in anger or the impact they had on my life.

A

July 29, 2021

The Young Man Who Didn't Want to be Drafted

Allow me to set the stage:

1. A young man, Logan Mailloux, was criminally convicted in Sweden last year for sharing an explicit photo of a woman performing a sex act, without her consent.
2. The Montreal Canadiens, specifically Marc Bergevin, drafted Logan Mailloux despite the defenseman's plea not to draft him.
3. Sponsors began jumping ship.
4. Geoff Molson said he didn't know Bergevin's plan to draft Logan Mailloux but is nonetheless remorseful and apologetic.
5. Geoff Molson also admits the Canadian organization made an error in judgment.
6. He promises the boy will go through a thorough re-education process in the years to come.

Photo by Markus Spiske on Unsplash

∞

Bad Judgement

If this was an ordinary organization, say a bank, and its general manager decided to hire a person who had been found guilty of a crime, the manager in question would have had to answer a few difficult questions from the head of the organization, such as:

1. What the hell were you thinking?
2. Oh! You're saying you weren't thinking! Is that it?
3. You also say you made a mistake, but that could happen to anyone?
4. And you're sorry?
5. You can stop apologizing. I got it. So what? Is that going to fix anything?
6. Let me ask you this: Are you sorry enough to quit? Or should I fire you?

A

July 30, 2021

Disarm Police!

"We are absolutely not saying that tomorrow morning, the police officers would not have a weapon," mayor Plante said, "...however, it must be done properly."

To help the mayor in her effort to disarm the Montreal Police Force, I propose 5 strategic occasions to disarm police officers appropriately:

1. During a cloudy day
2. During riots at Walmart
3. During a robbery at the public library
4. During a Chinese invasion of Ste-Catherine Street
5. During an alien attack anywhere on the planet

A

July 30, 2021

Warning

Apparently, someone found another way to hurt and insult people for no reason by hacking our Facebook pages. Here's a heads up to everyone! There's a hack on my Facebook page. It includes a hurtful sentence or inappropriate words that does not come from me.

If something shocking, inappropriate or indecent ever appears on my timeline, please know it didn't come from me. They'll use images, too.

I hope you all know that I would never send you anything unpleasant or rude. Those who know me, know that to be true.

A

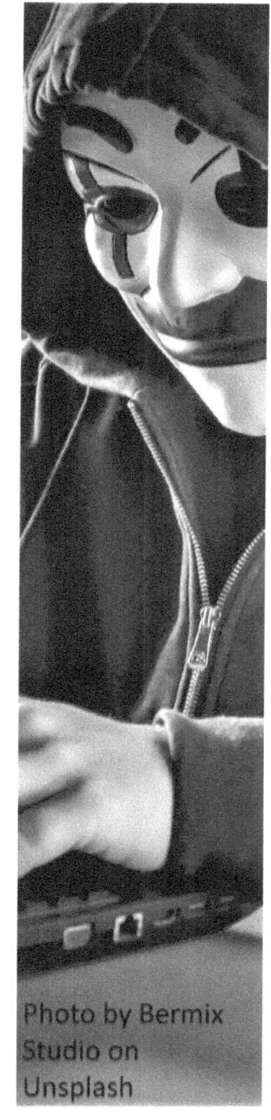

Photo by Bermix Studio on Unsplash

July 31, 2021

Dumbing Down Information with Silly Surveys

Unfortunately, every week, newspapers, in collaboration with survey firms, succeed in doing the impossible: how to manipulate ordinary information, which, by the way, does not deserve a second look, into a sensational Front Page.

This week, we're offered the following poll:

Who are the three women who have had the greatest impact on our history?

Judging by the survey results, it's obviously not the right title. It has been doctored, manipulated and adjusted to attract readers. The process is called dumbing down information for the masses. It's a deliberate oversimplification of intellectual content.

The real title should have been the following:

What are the first 3 names of women that come to mind?

Photo by Roman Kraft on Unsplash

This is a notoriety survey which by no means intends to measure historical significance.

Would you believe journalists often prefer to cover the spectacular rather than the important?

Yeah, you're right.

They're not really journalists.

A

August 1, 2021

Not Everything Is About You!

I've recently come across people I believed I knew well. They were intelligent, competent, educated, sound of mind and always helpful. Well, they found a way to surprise me. I thought I knew everything about them.

I suppose I got it wrong. I guess I'll need to upgrade my people-reading skills because I got a rude awakening these past few months. It appears not everyone understands the concept of living in a society and its responsibilities. For your information, this is what they told me:

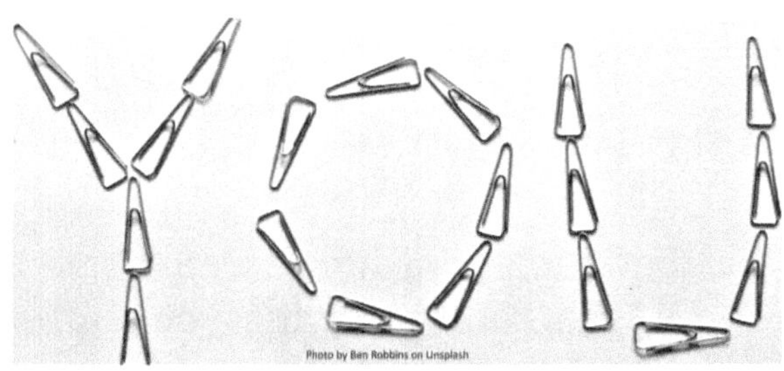

Photo by Ben Robbins on Unsplash

1. I don't believe I need to be vaccinated.
2. It's not for me.
3. It's too early to know if it's safe for me.
4. Don't need it, don't want it, no matter what you say, because I live in a free country.
5. I'd rather not talk about it.
6. Never been vaccinated. Why should I start now?
7. I don't want to get Covid-19 from the vaccine.

8. It's too much trouble getting to vaccine centers.
9. I don't have the time.
10. I've already had Covid-19, so I don't need to be vaccinated.
11. The vaccine might hurt me.
12. It's a personal thing.
13. It's none of your business if I don't get vaccinated.

It's Not about You!

Of course, the debate about getting vaccinated or not isn't new. That conversation has been around for years. And I understand why. Some are genuinely scared. Others, however, think only in terms of what do "I" want and how do "I" feel about getting vaccinated. It's all about the proverbial "me"! Not to burst anyone's bubble, but I have ground-breaking news. Information that needs to be heard and understood.

The Vaccine Is Not for You, It's for Us

Us, the people living and breathing around you.

Us, the people serving you dinner, delivering food to the supermarkets, cleaning your dishes.

Us, the people driving buses, taxis, the people teaching kids, caring for the sick, the cops, prosecutors and judges upholding the rule of law, students learning, businesses providing jobs, construction workers building the future, moms loving their children, artists nourishing our souls. I could go on and on. The list would cover a planet of "us".

Us, the planet that's waiting to be set free from the plague.

Look around you. "Us" means everyone around "you".

And that means you too!

A

August 17, 2021

Individuality Vs Vaccine: The Nitwit Battle of the Century

A veritable revelation came to me as I watched the news last night: how "no" became a hostile verb!

It was right there, in my face, staring at me for at least a year. And I couldn't see it.

What's this big revelation, you ask?

I finally understand why so many refuse to get vaccinated. It's not something new. It's not something that just popped into their heads. It's not fear or lack of empathy like we know it. The reason is simple and is anchored in childhood.

∞

Overactive Individuality

The anti-vaccine population reacts to everything it feels is being imposed on them. They possess a powerful sense of

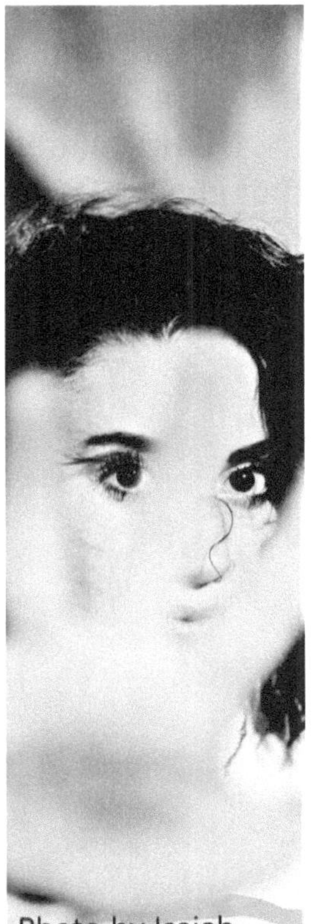

Photo by Isaiah Rustad on Unsplash

independence and, as a result, an overactive individuality. It posits that their freedom to choose is non-negotiable. They consider themselves islands unto themselves, living outside the boundaries of what is called the social contract: a theory that asserts that government exists only by the consent of the people in order to protect basic rights and promote the common good of society (John Locke 1632-1704).

I understand that everyone of us has that need to determine how we live our lives. It begins with that period in early childhood called the "terrible twos", when we practice and learn to say no! That's how we start building our identity. Some parents perceive their children's "no" as a hostile verb. It's not really. Luckily, most of us grow out of it. We refine our need to be independent, especially when "The needs of the many outweigh the needs of the few, or the one".

This awareness is a significant step on the path to becoming a mature adult.

Unfortunately for the rest of us, some have not been able to take that step. As a result, while we must treat them with respect, we must also exercise authority, just like we provide love, guidance, structure and discipline to young children.

A

August 27, 2021

Guns, Violent Shootouts and Blood on the Streets

Guns, the police chief and the mayor! That's who and what's in play.

Of course, you know there's a relationship between guns, the police and the current mayor. However, that said, what's really going on?

∞

Internal Conflicts

According to Montreal police chief Sylvain Caron's CV, he has 36 years of police experience, possesses strategic vision and is recognized by his peers as an effective manager.

Photo by Felix Koutchinski on Unsplash

He has a dual reporting relationship, one of whom is to Montreal mayor Valerie Plante.

Plante was born in Rouyn-Noranda. In 1994, she moved to Montreal to attend university, receiving a degree in anthropology and another in museology (the study of museums).

Our Security

The current mayor is presently thinking about how to disarm the police force and redirecting funds toward services that are, according to Mayor Plante, better suited to satisfy the needs of citizens.

Chief Caron is most likely thinking about how the recent violence involving guns will impact Montreal citizens, his police force and mayor Plante's re-election in November.

My Question

I wonder what I would do if I was police chief and had to deal with gunfire nearly every other day, a museologist/mayor every single day, the same one that's willing to put Caron's officers in harm's way and, his police rank and file.

Are you thinking what I'm thinking?

Probably not.

Try again.

A

August 28, 2021

Wars and Resiliency

As a people, we're not as resilient as we would like to be. Perhaps it's because we didn't need to before the pandemic. But, like others around the world, we have had to find ways to be resilient during the Covid-19 pandemic.

Those who suffered through wars didn't have a choice. If they wanted to survive, they had to be resilient, tough and perseverant. They had to be tenacious and keep trying, no matter what.

Many countries have experienced wars in their own land and, not surprisingly, their people had to find ways to continue their lives and endure, to live in a stressful environment and to persevere against all odds.

Because of their histories, are they more resilient today than we are? That's a good question.

The answer is... I don't know. What I do know is that some of us are going through a pretty tough time.

To help you think about this, here is an abridged list of countries that have experienced

war(s), revolutions and insurrections first-hand between 1803 and 2011. They include:

Indonesia 1803–1837
Texas 1812–1813,1819, 1821,1826–1827, 1835–1836, 1838, 1905, 1905
Argentina 1814–1880, 1890, 1893, 1893, 1955
South Africa 1817–1819
Greece 1824–1825, 1946–1949
Portugal 1828–1834
Chile 1829–1830, 1851, 1891
Egypt 1831–1833
Spain 1833–1839, 1846–1849, 1872–1876, 1936–1939, 1939–1965
Brazil 1835–1845, 1896–1897, 1932
New Mexico 1837
Uruguay 1839–1851
Yucatán 1841–1848
California 1846
Switzerland 1847
China 1851–1863, 1899–1901,1912–1928, 1927–1937, 1945–1949
Kansas 1854–1858
Australia 1854
Utah 1857–1858
Mexico 1857–1861, 1910–1920, 1926–1929
Malaysia 1857–1863, 1968–1989
Venezuela 1859–1863, 1901–1903
United States 1861–1865
Germany1866, 1878, 1918–1919
Malaysia 1867–1874, 1948–1960, 1962–1990
Japan 1868–1869, 1877
Canada 1885
Central America1898–1934

Bolivia 1899
Colombia 1899–1902, 1947
Persia 1905–1911
Russia 1917–1923, 1939–1945, 1989, 2008
Iraq 1918–2003
Finland 1918
Ukraine 1917-1921, 1943–1956
Turkey 1919–1922
Ireland 1922–1923
Paraguay 1922–1923, 1947
Nicaragua 1926–1927, 1962–1990
Austria 1934-1945
World War 1, 1914-1918 Germany, Austria-Hungary,
Bulgaria, the Ottoman Empire, Great Britain, France,
Russia, Italy, Romania, Japan and the United States
World War 2, 1939–1945 China, Czechoslovakia,
Austria, Poland, Denmark, Norway, Belgium, Japan,
The Netherlands, France, Britain – the Channel Islands,
Soviet Union, United States, Italy
Yugoslavia 1941–1945, 1991–1999
Italy 1943–1945
Poland 1944–1947, 1963
Iran 1946, 1945–1946
Romania 1947–1962
Palestine 1947–1948
Costa Rica 1948
Israel 1947–1949, 1950s–1960, 1956, 1967, 1967–1970,
1973, 1971–1982, 1982, 1985–2000, 1987–1993, 2000–
2005, 2006, 2008–2009, 2012, 2014
Myanmar 1948–
Korea 1950–1953
Cuba 1953–1959
Laos 1953–1975

Vietnam 1946–1955, 1955–1975
Sudan 1955–1972, 1983–2005
Congo 1960–1966, 1996–1997, 1997–1999, 1998–2003
Guatemala 1960–1996
Yemen 1962–1970, 1986, 1994, 2015–
Dominican Republic 1965
Rhodesia 1965–1980
Thailand 1965–1983
Cyprus 1963–1964
Cambodia 1967–1975, 1997
Nigeria 1967–1970
Northern Ireland 1960–1998
Bangladesh 1971
Ethiopia 1974–1991
Lebanon 1975–1990
Mozambique 1975–1992
Angola 1961–1974, 1976–2002
El Salvador1979–1992
Peru 1980–1993
Sri Lanka 1983–2009
Afghanistan 1989–1992, 1978, 1992–1996, 1996–2001
Liberia 1989–1996, 1999–2003
Rwanda 1990–1994
Senegal 1990–2006
Georgia 1991–1993
Iraq 1991, 1994–1997, 2006–2009
Sierra Leone 1991–2002
Yugoslavia 1991- 2001
Algeria 1991–2002
Tajikistan 1992–1997
Burundi 1993–2005
Nepal 1996–2006
Albania 1997

Guinea-Bissau 1998–1999
Libya 2011, 2014–2020
Syria 2011–

A

September 8, 2021

Buried Children

The remains of 215 children found buried near a residential school: why that doesn't surprise me.

The jury is still out, but finding 215 native children, probably kidnapped from their homes, buried near a residential school, could be the result of a crime, possibly a genocide.

The school was run by the Catholic Church from the late 19th century to the late 1970s when the federal government took it over. I expect we will find more of such horror stories from British Columbia to Newfoundland.

Let me be candid and utterly unfair to those clerics that believe in God and truly help people every day. The Catholic Church as well as other religions have, through the years, waged wars, murdered, tortured and abused men, women and children. My feelings toward these organizations run the gamut from horror to unmerciful. These feelings have been growing as I matured over time.

Truth be told, whenever I come in contact with a cleric, my skin crawls. My mind prompts an immediate defense mechanism: to run away

Photo by Mwesigwa
Joel on Unsplash

because I'm probably not dealing with an honest or sane person.

Having been brought up as a Catholic, I have experienced firsthand what good clerics can do to help a young man make the right decisions and develop courage and resilience. I've also witnessed the "others" who, I'm afraid to say, chose religion to hurt people. They are either unfit to guide other people's lives or, I'm sorry to say, are sociopaths and are unfit to be human beings.

As you can imagine, Pope Francis is facing a difficult job in trying to reform his own people and the Vatican.

The most significant issue facing religious societies is about supervising their own people. It's a fatal flaw in any organization.

Unfortunately, our story is not only about children. It's about criminals that we've chosen, trained and promoted in our society.

Can you imagine what these innocent children went through? Visualize your son or daughter being kidnapped before your very eyes and placed under the authority of criminals. Close your eyes and imagine what you see and feel.

When I think about it, I really don't want another apology from the Church. I want justice for those children and their families.

A

More books by André John Haddad

*Available at Amazon, Barnes & Noble, Indigo,
and other major online book retailers.*

An industrial psychologist since 1974, André John Haddad has designed and facilitated shifts in resources and business strategies in Europe, the Americas and Asia. His alternative concepts and methods have helped thousands of people navigate large organizations, understand and predict customer behavior, improve performance and accelerate development. André is also the creator of an innovation process for entrepreneurs that has been part of an Executive MBA program since 2008.

In addition to *Five Hundred Days of Killer Viruses and Attempted Wit*, André is also the author of the fictional works *The Jerusalem Cycle* trilogy and *The Thirst*.